A Warning to Sinners to Flee from the Wrath to Come

By Nathaniel Vincent

A Warning to Sinners to Flee from the Wrath to Come
By Nathaniel Vincent

Edited by C. Matthew McMahon and Therese B. McMahon
Transcribed by Blake Gentry

Changes made to this edition do not affect the overall language of the document, nor do they change the writer's intention. Spelling, grammar, and formatting changes have been made, and modernized wording is used in specific cases to help today's reader more fully grasp the intention of the author.

© 2012 by Puritan Publications and A Puritan's Mind

Published by Puritan Publications
A Ministry of A Puritan's Mind
4101 Coral Tree Circle #214
Coconut Creek, FL 33073
www.puritanpublications.com
www.apuritansmind.com
www.puritanshop.com

All rights reserved. No part of this publication may be reproduced, stored in a retrieval system or transmitted in any form by any means, electronic, mechanical, photocopy, recording or otherwise, without the prior permission of the publisher, except as provided by USA copyright law.

First Electronic Edition, 2012
First Modern Print Edition, 2012
Manufactured in the United States of America

eISBN: 978-1-938721-56-4
ISBN: 978-1-938721-57-1

A Warning to Sinners to Flee from the Wrath to Come

TABLE OF CONTENTS

MEET NATHANIEL VINCENT 4
[ORIGINAL TITLE PAGE] 10
THE EPISTLE TO THE READER 11
CHAPTER 1: THE TEXT OPENED 14
CHAPTER 2: THE MAIN DOCTRINE OF THE TEXT 17
CHAPTER 3: THE JUDGE 19
CHAPTER 4: THE PEOPLE TO BE JUDGED 24
CHAPTER 5: THINGS TO BE JUDGED 31
CHAPTER 6: THE CERTAINTY OF JUDGMENT 38
CHAPTER 7: APPLICATION OF THE WARNING 42
CHAPTER 8: THE DAMNATION OF HELL 58
CHAPTER: TURN TO GOD OR TURN INTO HELL 63
CHAPTER 9: SIN THAT BESETS US 88
CHAPTER 10: APPLICATION TO WILLINGLY HAVE SUCH SIN DISCOVERED 105

MEET NATHANIEL VINCENT

[Vincent's Portrait by John White (1681) from the National Portrait Gallery]

Nathaniel Vincent (1639?-1697), nonconformist puritan divine, was probably born in Cornwall about 1639 (*cf. epist. Dedication* to *A Present for such as have been Sick*).

His father, John Vincent (1591-1646), son and heir of Thomas Vincent of Northill, Cornwall, born in 1591, matriculated from New College, Oxford, on Dec. 15, 1609, became a student at Lincoln's Inn in 1612, and, afterwards taking orders, was beneficed in Cornwall. Of nonconformist leanings, he was driven there by his bishop, as well as from so many other livings that it was said no two of his seven children were born in the same county. Coming to London in 1642, he was nominated by the committee of the Westminster assembly to the rich rectory of Sedgefield, Durham, but died after holding it but two years, in 1646. His widow, Sarah Vincent, petitioned on Nov. 1, 1656 and in April 1657 for 60l. which her husband had lent to the parliament (Cal. *State Papers*, Dom. 1656, pp. 146, 147, 185, 191, 329; Addit. MS. 15671, cf. ff. 38, 42, 55, 69, 114, 124, 140, 148, 150, 219, 227, 238, 251). Their eldest son, John, who inherited his grandfather's estate of Northill, is confused by Mr. Wood with a son of Augustine Vincent (*Athenæ Oxon.* vol. i. p. xxxv). The second son, Thomas, is separately noticed.

Nathaniel, the third son, entered Oxford University as a chorister on Oct. 18, 1648, at age 10. He matriculated from Corpus Christi College on March 28, 1655, graduated with a B.A. from Christ Church on March 13, 1655-6, M. A. on June 11, 1657, and was chosen chaplain of Corpus Christi College. He was appointed by Cromwell one of the first fellows of Durham University, but never lived there. At twenty he was preaching at Pulborough, Sussex, and at twenty-one was ordained and presented to the rectory of Langley Marish, Buckinghamshire. There he was ejected on St. Bartholomew's day, 1662, after which he lived three years as chaplain to Sir Henry and Lady Blount at Tittenhanger, Hertfordshire. About 1666 Vincent went to London. There his preaching at once attracted attention, and a meeting-house was shortly built for him in Farthing Alley, Southwark, where he gathered a large congregation. In spite of fines and rough handling by soldiers sent to drag him from his pulpit, he continued boldly preaching during the stormy times. In July 1670, soon after his marriage, he was confined in the Marshalsea prison. He was removed to the Gatehouse, Westminster, on Aug. 22 (*cf.* Cal. State Papers, Dom., Addenda, 1660-70, p. 546). He remained six months in prison. In 1682 he was again arrested, brought before magistrates at Dorking, and sentenced to three years' imprisonment, after which he was to be banished from the country. A flaw, however, was perceived in the indictment, and, after the section expenditure of 200*l.*, Vincent was released, but so weakened from illness that he was long unable to preach (Letter to his Congregation, 24 June 1683). He was again arrested in February 1686, this time on an improbable charge of being concerned in Monmouth's rebellion (Wood, Life and Times, ed. Clark, iii. 179). Some of his books were written in prison; thus "his pen was going when his tongue could not."

Vincent died suddenly on June 22, 1697, in the fifty-ninth year of his age. He was buried at Bunhill Fields; (see *Inscriptions on Tombs in Bunhill Fields*, 1717, p. 34). His funeral sermon was preached by Nathaniel Taylor.

Wood's *encomium* on Vincent is unusually high, "He was of smarter, more brisk, and florid parts than most of his dull and sluggish fraternity can reasonably pretend to; of a facetious and jolly humour, and a considerable scholar."

The *works* of Nathaniel Vincent are as follows:

1. *The Doctrine of Conversion*, or, *The Conversion of a Sinner Explained and Applied*, London, 1669, 8vo; with which is published 2. *The Day of Grace* (same date). 3. *A Covert from the Storm*, London, 1671, 8vo (written in prison). 4. *The Spirit of Prayer*, London, 1674, 8vo; republished, 1677, 8vo; 5th edit. 1699; other edits. Saffron Walden, ed. J. H. Hopkins, 1815, London, 1825. 5. *A Heaven or Hell on Earth*, London, 1676, 8vo. 6. *The Little Child's Catechism*, whereunto is added several Short Histories, 1681, 12mo. 7. *The True Touchstone*, London, 1681, 8vo. 8. *The More*

Excellent Way, London, 1684. 9. *A Warning given to secure Sinners*, London, 1688, 8vo. 10. *The Principles of the Doctrine of Christ. a Catechism*, London, 1691, 8vo. 11. *A Present for such as have been Sick* (sermons preached after his recovery from sickness), London, 1693. 12. *The Cure of Distractions in attending on God*. 13. *The Love of the World cured*. 14. *Worthy Walking*. The dates of the last three do not appear. Sermons by Vincent are in Annesley's Continuation of *Morning Exercises*, London, 1683, and in his *Casuistical Morning Exercises*, London, 1690; reprinted in vols. iv., v., and vi. of Nichols's edition, London, 1814-5, 8vo. Vincent was much in request for preaching funeral sermons; five or six were printed in quarto. He edited the *Morning Exercise against Popery* (London, 1675, 4to), twenty-five sermons preached in his pulpit at Southwark by eminent divines.

For further study:

Clark's *Indexes*, vol. ii. pt. i. p. 280, pt. ii. p. 308; Foster's Alumni (1500-1714); Neal's Puritans, iii. 521; Calamy's Continuation, i. 30; *Alumni Westmon.* p. 129; Burrows's *Visitation*, pp. 171, 173, 369, 477; Bloxam's *Reg. of Magd. Coll.* v. 208; Palmer's *Nonconf. Mem.* i. 304; Wood's *Athenae Oxon.* iv. 617; Wilson's *Hist. of Diss. Churches*, iv. 304 (this is the most accurate account); Cal. *State Papers*, Dom. Add. 1660-70 pp. 273, 388, 464, 1671 p. 556; Taylor's Funeral

Sermon, 1697, 4to; Wood's *Life and Times* (Oxford Hist. Soc.), ii. 561; *Hist. MSS. Comm.* 11th Rep. App. p 46; *Notes and Queries*, 2nd ser. ix. 267.

Taken in part from the National Dictionary of Biography, public domain.

[ORIGINAL TITLE PAGE]

A
WARNING
GIVEN TO
Secure Sinners,
TO
Prepare for *judgment*,
TO
flee from wrath to come,
AND
turn from all sin;
BUT
Especially the sin which *most easily besets them*.

BY NATHANIEL VINCENT, M.A.
Minister of the Gospel.

Ezek. 33:7, "O Son of Man, I have set thee a watchman unto the house of Israel, therefore thou shalt hear the Word at my mouth, and warn them from me."

Licensed, March 17th, 1688.

LONDON,
Printed by *J. Atwood* for *Thomas Parkhurst* at the *Bible* and *three Crowns*, at the lower end of *Cheapside*, near *Mercer's Chapel*, 1688.

A Warning to Sinners to Flee from the Wrath to Come

THE EPISTLE TO THE READER

Reader,

When I preached these following sermons, I did not have the least thought of publishing them. They were taken from my mouth by a dexterous and nimble hand that wrote almost every word I uttered. I was solicited very much to print them; and the notes have been written out fairly, and brought to me. I have looked them over, and now they are presented to you with a sincere design that they may be beneficial to you, and that they will not be without hope. The subjects handled here are awakening; and in this secure age, there is a great need of startling sermons! At this day in England, there is enough work for many *Boanerges*, for many sons of thunder.

    The guilt and defilement of sin proves it to be man's greatest enemy; but because it stupefies and hardens those that have been guilty of it, it is likely to effectually destroy them; for since the disease is not felt, the remedy is neglected. A spiritual lethargy is the general distemper, most continue fast asleep in sin, until hell wakes them, but then it is too late. Though Christ has the key of hell, the Savior does not release any that are thrown into it. Miserable world, because it lies in wickedness! More miserable, because it does not apprehend how miserable its wickedness has made it! Because it does not fear, it does not endeavor to escape eternal misery!

O! dreadful day of God that is coming, when all apostate angels that are now in chains of darkness, shall be brought forth and judged, and dealt with as the enemies of God and man. These principalities and powers will be overthrown, and utterly unable to avoid the severity of their righteous and almighty Judge. How much evil they have done, and still they are doing more! Of what woe and torment are they capable!

And all those of the children of men who have been led captive by Satan, at his pleasure, that have resolved rather to be destroyed than for the works of the devil to be destroyed in them, it is just that they should, but how sad it will be for them to share in torment with him! Sin will have a very bad end; all that have gone into another world are sensible of it, though few in this world perceive it. When the servants of sin have received their wages, which is death, then they will know their sorrow, what kind of master they have served, and what pains they foolishly took for that misery, which they should have taken pains to have prevented.

A Warning to Sinners to Flee from the Wrath to Come

Reader! Be wise, believe and fear, and take the *watchman's* warning. The sword in the hand of the living and eternal God will give a dreadful and deadly blow and to fall under his vengeance will be fearful; and your blood lies on your own head; it will lie very heavily, and on this will follow everlasting heaviness and anguish. O! fear the wrath to come before it has come, and fly away from sin, and come to God by Jesus Christ, a Savior from both sin and wrath, and a Savior to the uttermost. Better counsel than this cannot be received by yourself, nor given to you by another.

Nathaniel Vincent

CHAPTER 1:
THE TEXT OPENED

"We shall stand before the judgment seat of Christ," (Romans 14:10).

I have been lately discoursing concerning conversion. The digression I make this day is subservient to my great design, which is the conversion and salvation of this assembly. It infinitely concerns you all to turn to God, for you will quickly have a summons to come to his judgment seat, and who can tell how soon that summons may be given? Those that think it least, and least care to be provided and ready for it, perhaps may have it soonest; and if the converts themselves, as the Scripture tells us, are scarcely saved, where shall the unconverted and the sinner appear? I wish that I may preach and you may hear, as those who truly believe that we shall all stand before the judgment seat of Christ.

The apostle speaks enough in these words, one would think, to startle the most stupid conscience, to make the most secure, like Felix, tremble; to awaken even those that are dead in sins and trespasses. Let me tell you, none of the devils are atheists and infidels, for they all believe this text, and the thoughts of judgment make them tremble. Therefore, if any sinner remains fearless and insensible, in this respect, he even out-sins the apostate angels.

There are three things observable in the *words of my text*,

1. Here is a judgment seat, the most glorious that ever was, the last that ever will be; from this tribunal there can be no appeal to any other, the sentence, whether of absolution or condemnation, that are passed here, will never be reversed, but stand firm through *eternity*.

2. You are told who is to be the Judge, he is the Lord Jesus Christ. We read of a twofold appearing of Christ, his first and his second appearing. He came at first in the form of a servant, he was to be made sin, and he was made sin and a curse for us. He gave himself for us, that he might redeem us from all iniquity; and if he had given something other than or less than himself, it would not have satisfied. The church's sins could be done away with by no lower a Priest, than Christ, the greatest and highest of all; and the Priest was glad to be Priest, and that a most voluntary sacrifice. He appeared at first to put away sin by the sacrifice of himself, but when he comes the second time, to judge the world, he will appear after another kind of manner. From the beginning of the world, there has not been such a sight as there will be at the end of it. The Lord Jesus will come with a power which none can withstand, with great glory, which will fill the saints with

Chapter 1: The Test Opened

joy; for they shall appear in glory with him, but will be exceedingly amazing and confounding to all those who were the enemies of his kingdom.

3. Here are the persons that are to stand before this Judge. If you ask, who are they? I answer by another question, who, or where are the persons that shall be exempted? All from the beginning of the world, to the end of it, all from the first man that was made, to the last of his posterity that shall be born, must stand before Christ the Lord, that from his mouth they may receive their final and eternal doom. There is a great difference between standing before the judgment seat, and standing in judgment; the former implies being made to appear at the tribunal, the latter implies being acquitted there. The psalmist tells us, "That the ungodly shall not stand in the judgment, nor sinners in the congregation of the righteous," (Psalm 1:5) yet all of these shall be forced to appear at the judgment seat of God, there they shall stand trembling, expecting the terrible sentence of condemnation. And O! what a hideous outcry will the whole multitude of wicked and reprobate ones make when they are judged to endless misery without hope of mercy!

CHAPTER 2:
MAIN DOCTRINE OF THE TEXT

DOCTRINE. The doctrine I raise from the words is this, *All shall be judged by Christ at the great day.* As certainly as you are all here, so certainly at that day you shall appear at his judgment seat. Death is not more certain, no, it is not so certain as judgment. The apostle tells us that all shall not die, for some shall be changed; but even these that are changed, though they escape the grave, they shall stand at the tribunal and give account of themselves to God. This doctrine concerning judgment was preached early in the world. We find it was published before the flood of Noah, as you may see in Jude, verses 14-15, where you have the sum of a sermon, but a very terrible one, preached by Enoch, the seventh from Adam, "Behold the Lord cometh with ten thousands of his saints, to execute judgment on all; and to convince all that are ungodly among them, of all their ungodly deeds which they have ungodly committed, and of all the hard speeches which ungodly sinners have spoken against him." Under the Mosaic dispensation, the children of Israel heard the same doctrine.

Chapter 2: The Main Doctrine of the Text

That great prince and preacher, Solomon, in this way concludes his book of Ecclesiastes, having displayed the creature's vanity, having taught man his interest and duty, to fear God, and to keep his commandments; he closes with these words, "God will bring every work into judgment, with every secret thing, whether it be good, or whether it be evil," (Ecclesiastes 12:14). And how plainly does the apostle Paul speak to the same purpose, "For we must all appear before the judgment seat of Christ, that everyone may receive the things done in his body, according to what he hath done, whether it be good or bad; knowing therefore the terror of the Lord, we persuade men," (2 Corinthians 5:10-11).

In the handling of this doctrine, this is the method I shall *observe*:

First, I shall discourse concerning He that is the Judge.

Secondly, I shall speak concerning the people that are to be judged.

Thirdly, concerning the things that shall be brought into judgment.

Fourthly, I shall demonstrate the certainty of this judgment.

Lastly, make application.

CHAPTER 3:
THE JUDGE

In the first place, I am to discourse concerning the Judge, and the text plainly tells us that the Judge is *Christ*. I grant that the Father is said to judge, "If ye call on the Father, who without respect of persons judgeth according to every man's work, pass the time of your sojourning here in fear," (1 Peter 1:17). Yet it is said in another place, "The Father judgeth no man, but hath committed all judgment to the Son," (John 5:22). How shall theses Scriptures be reconciled? The reconciliation is easy in this way; the Father judges, because the authority of judging belongs to him, because he consents to the Son's judgment, and has ordained him to judge the world in righteousness; the truth is, the Father judges all, but it is immediately by Jesus Christ. And yet in another sense, the Father does not judge, because Christ the Son, the second Person in the Godhead alone, was incarnate and manifested in the flesh, and he alone will visibly judge the world at the great approaching day.

These four things may be observed concerning Christ the Judge:

He is a Savior to the uttermost.

He is the only Savior.

He is Lord of all.

And as such a Lord, he will come with a most glorious attendance.

1. Christ the Judge is a Savior to the uttermost, and truly at judgment day, he will complete the church's salvation; he began it here in this world, and is still carrying it on; but the last day will be the day, in which he will put his last hand to this work, and make it perfect, "Christ was once offered up to bear the sins of many, and unto them that look for him shall he appear the second time, without sin to salvation," (Hebrews 9:28); then salvation shall be consummate, the whole of it shall be wrought, nothing of sin or the sad effects of it shall remain, nothing that shall cause the least frown in the face of God to eternity. Death will be swallowed up in victory, the whole man will be glorious and immortal; Christ will then have completed his whole design on all his saints and members, he will have made them as holy and happy as he intended to make them, he will indeed "present his church a glorious church, not having spot or wrinkle, or any such thing; but it shall be all holy, and its beauty without the least blemish," (Ephesians 5:27).

2. Christ the Judge is the only Savior, therefore for those that are condemned by him, it is a vain thought for them

to expect salvation from any other. Christ is the only foundation stone on which all that build shall stand; other builders are foolish, and build on the sand, and what they build will fall, and the fall of it will be great. Those that are not interested in the Lord Jesus by faith, that are not justified by his blood, who besides can save them from wrath? Those whose iniquities are not done away by his offering up of himself without spot to God, there can be no other sacrifice found for their sins, but a certain fearful looking for of judgment, and fiery indignation that shall devour the adversaries. And how dreadful will it be to be sentenced to death and damnation, by the only Author of salvation and life! Those that shall be doomed by his mouth to eternal destruction, that destruction will be made ten thousand times sorer by eternal desperation. Alas, what hope can be left, when the Lamb of God, who alone can take away sin, shall be so full of wrath, as forever to reject and cast away the sinner?

3. Christ the Judge is Lord of all; this is a truth that the tongue of an angel proclaimed, (Luke 2:11) a truth that "every tongue should confess," (Philippians 2:11) that every heart ought to believe, and which the most unbelieving and obstinate at last shall be made to know. Christ has on his "vesture, and on his thigh, this Name written, King of Kings, and Lord of Lords," (Revelation 19:16). He has all power in his

Chapter 3: The Judge

hand, things in heaven, and earth, and under the earth are subject to him. Those that are wise willingly bow before him, and those who will not bow, he can easily break and dash to pieces. A mighty Lord Christ is, at whose command death shall deliver again all that for so many years he had imprisoned in the grace; he indeed has the key of death and hell too, (Revelation 1:18) both are under his power; also at his command "the heavens shall pass away with a great noise, the elements shall melt with fervent heat, the earth also and the works therein shall be burnt up." There is no dealing with this Judge by way of resistance; it concerns us all to be diligent, "that we may be found of him in peace, without spot and blameless," (2 Peter 3:10, 14).

4. Christ the Judge will come with a most glorious attendance. How awakening to the world will the voice of the arch angel and the trump of God be! Christ will appear with a light far above the brightness of the sun, and shall shine like that glorious luminary, "Then shall the righteous shine as the sun in the kingdom of their Father," (Matthew 13:43). And what a spectacle will all the saints be together, as so many millions of suns shining at once, and their Lord in the height of glory at the head of them! He will be revealed also with his mighty angels; these excellent spirits at his command, ministered to his members on earth, and they will wait on the

head at the day of his appearing and his kingdom. There is much work for the angels to do at the world's end, they are compared to reapers that are safely to gather the wheat, and to bind the tares in bundles for the fire. "The Son of Man shall send forth his angels, and they shall gather out of his kingdom all things that offend, and them which do iniquity, and shall cast them into a furnace of fire; there shall be weeping and gnashing of teeth," (Matthew 13:41-42). The greatest train of nobility and courtiers that attend at the coronation of the highest emperor on earth, are a poor show to an innumerable company of angels; for all heaven will be with Christ at the judgment, to do him honor, who is indeed the head of all principality and power. So much for the doctrine pertaining to Jesus Christ the Judge.

CHAPTER 4:
THE PEOPLE TO BE JUDGED

In the second place, I am to speak of the people that are to be judged. The text says *in all*; therefore none shall be exempted, and none in a vain and foolish imagination should exempt themselves. It will be a general assize, at which all the sons and daughters of Adam shall appear.

1. The highest and greatest of men will be brought to judgment. Death makes bold with them as well as others, and enters the stateliest palaces, the strongest forts, as well as the cottages of the meanest. The rulers and conquerors of the world, that caused terror in the land of the living, they are made to bear the shame of their weakness and mortality; they are brought down to the pit, their swords are laid under their heads, their hands being able to hold them no longer, (Ezekiel 32:27). And if death is not afraid to seize them, surely Christ will not be afraid to judge them. This mighty Lord "regards not the persons of princes, nor the rich more than the poor," (Job 34:19). "I have said ye are gods," speaking to the great ones of the world, "but ye shall die like men," (Psalm 82:7). Princes are greater worms, other men are lesser, but all must call corruption their father; and when they come to stand before Christ's bar, foregoing earthly dignity will be

insignificant, all must stand on even ground. And truly those great ones of the world that have abused their power, and by a bad example drawn many to sin and to hell after them, their greatness will only increase their account and misery.

2. As the greatest, so the meanest must be brought to judgment, though there is never so vast a multitude; God takes notice of them all now, and none of them must think to escape in a crowd then. The apostle speaks plainly of individuals, "So then everyone of us shall give account of himself to God," (Romans 14:12). Those that live most private and retired, are under God's continual inspection; those that are of the lowest rank and quality, whom, there are that disdain so much as to look on, yet God sees them. The sun shines on a mole hill as well as on a mountain, on a shrub as well as on a cedar, on a fly as well as on an emperor; and truly the all-seeing eye of God beholds the low as well as the high, and all of them shall be made to render an account of all his doings.

3. Righteous ones must stand before Christ's judgment seat. All his members must appear before him, their head, but shall be dealt with after a different manner from others. Grace and love makes a difference now, but how highly magnified will the grace of Christ be in the difference it makes on that day? To find the mercy of the Lord on that day, which the

apostle prays Onesiphorus might find, (2 Timothy 1:18) when the greatest part of the world shall be struck with a strong hand, the earth being deaf to all their cries, be turned into everlasting fire; this is great mercy indeed, great as the heaven is high above the earth. The righteous shall appear, but they shall be set at their Lord's right hand, to show his peculiar favor to them, and they shall joyfully own what that hand has done for them. Christ's appearing will be glorious, and so will be the appearing of his saints; then it will be understood what it is to be a saint, "When Christ who is our life shall appear, then shall ye also appear with him in glory," (Colossians 3:4).

A question is started here by some, whether the sins of the righteous shall be made known then? The Scripture plainly tells us, that when the sins of such come to be sought for, there shall be none, and they shall not be found; none of them shall be imputed or laid to their charge, none shall be so discovered in judgment, as to rise up in judgment against them, to condemn them. But since there will be such a light shining on that day that will make all things manifest, both good and evil, suppose the iniquities of the righteous should be made known to the whole creation, such will be their purity, such will be their blessedness and joy, that there will not be the least room for shame or sorrow at the discovery. But when all the sins that have been forgiven and purged shall be revealed, others as well as themselves will be filled with wonder at the blood of Jesus, and the powerful grace of God.

4. As the righteous, so the wicked must stand before Christ's bar; they would gladly not come near, but there is an irresistible power to force them. The malefactor who is condemned for murder, rape, or treason, would gladly decline the Judge's view, he is self-condemned, and therefore fears the Judge's sentence; but the jailer, the officers compel him to the bar, where judgment is given against him to take away his life. Wicked men will be horribly afraid to make their appearance before the Lord Jesus, whose salvation they have slighted, whose kingdom and government they would by no means submit to. They will wish that their bodies might sleep eternally in their graves, and never have such a resurrection which will be only to damnation. They will wish rather to be turned into nothing, than to be turned into hell. They will "call to the rocks and the mountains to fall on them, to hide them from the face of him that sits on the throne, and from the wrath of the Lamb," (Revelation 6:16). But they must appear at his seat regardless of whether they want to or not, and see him eye to eye, though his eye will be as a flame of fire to terrify them. That just indignation that sparkles from Christ's looks, how will it amaze them! "Behold he cometh with clouds, and every eye shall see him, and all the kindreds of the

earth shall wail because of him, even so amen," (Revelation 1:7); the thing is *certain*.

5. Those that never heard Christ's Gospel shall be brought to judgment. He is to judge the church, and the whole world in righteousness. The state of those that are without the Gospel, is set forth as *very sad* in the Scriptures. They are said to be "without Christ, being aliens from the commonwealth of Israel, and strangers to the covenants of promise, having no hope, and without God in the world, (Ephesians 2:12). Yet it seems to me an unwarrantable boldness, to pronounce them all lost; since for all we know, God may help some of them to be faithful in that little he has given to them. But however, whether it is or not, their case is so dangerous, that we should be concerned very much for them at present, and pray that God would make known his saving power among them. The apostle tells us, what will be the rule of Christ's proceedings with the heathen, that never heard the glad tidings of salvation. They shall be judged according to the law and light of nature. "As many as have sinned without law, shall also perish without law, and as many as have sinned in the law, shall be judged by the law; for not the hearers of the law are just before God, but the doers of the law shall be justified," (Romans 2:12).

6. Those that have enjoyed the Gospel, and the means of grace, shall be brought to judgment, and of all people that are to be judged, these have the largest account to give and the most talents to answer for. A poor heathen, he has only one talent, the dim light of nature. But you that enjoy the Gospel have two, if not five talents to improve. And where much is given, will not much also be required. You that hear Christ preached, had need to look to it, that you sincerely obey him now and that you may stand before him at last. For if you fall in judgment, you will fall very low. Damnation will be great and extraordinary, where great salvation has been neglected, (Hebrews 2:3). Our Lord Jesus plainly intimates, that there are degrees of torment in the place of future punishment. There is a blacker darkness, and a darkness not quite so dismal. There is a cooler and a hotter hell. Who are those that shall be thrown into the hottest hell of all? Truly those who heard the Gospel, and were called to repent and believe, but would do neither. "Woe unto thee Chorazin, woe unto thee Bethsaida, for if the mighty works that were done in you, had been done in Tyre and Sidon, they would have repented long ago in sackcloth and ashes; but I say to you, it shall be more tolerable for Tyre and Sidon in the day of judgment, than for you. And thou Capernaum, that are exalted unto heaven, shalt be cast down to hell; for if the mighty works which have been

Chapter 4: The People to be Judged

done in thee, had been done in Sodom, it would have remained to this day. But I say to you, it shall be more tolerable for the land of Sodom in the day of judgment, than for thee," (Matthew 11:21-24).

CHAPTER 5:
THINGS TO BE JUDGED

In the third place, I am to speak of the things which will be brought into judgment, with respect to both the righteous and the wicked.

I begin with the righteous, and concerning these you must *know*:

1. Their sincerity at the Day of Judgment, will be made apparent. All the sincerity that has been on earth, will then be owned and approved. Everyone shall have a *euge*, a commendation, that has been a good and faithful servant, (Matthew 25:21, 23). The apostle prays for the Philippians, that they "might be sincere, and without offense till the day of Christ," (Philippians 1:10). Sincerity will signify much in that day. None will pass for sincere, but those that truly are so. All that have been sincere shall be accepted and rewarded. Faithful ones may now possibly be loaded with reproaches from outside, and with censures from within the church. But at the great day, all will be wiped off. "Judge nothing before the time, until the Lord do come, who both will bring to light the hidden things of darkness, and make manifest the counsels of the hearts, and then shall every man have praise of

God," (1 Corinthians 4:5). How many that have been highly esteemed among men, will be discovered then to have been unsound at heart, and that the world and themselves acted and ruled them, though their tongues did speak for God, and though they made a splendid profession, that they were his servants. And how many that have been hardly thought of by men, will Christ confess before his Father and the angels on that day? Their censurers at the same time will be their shame and confoundment.

2. Cognizance will be taken of all the good works of the righteous. These will follow them into another world, (Revelation 14:13). The apostle, that he might encourage believers to diligence, tells them, "God is not unrighteous to forget your work and labor of love, which ye have shewed towards his Name," (Hebrews 6:10). Good works are rewardable, though they are not meritorious. There is no proportion between the work and the reward, but the reward infinitely exceeds, for God himself is the reward of the saints, and all in all that are in heaven. There is no intrinsic worth in good works to deserve heaven. But God has promised heaven and eternal life, and is righteous in bestowing it. But still it must be acknowledged as his free gift, and given through Jesus Christ. Indeed mention is made only of works of charity and mercy, "I was hungry, and ye gave me meat, thirsty and ye

gave me drink, I was a stranger, and ye took me in. I was naked, and ye clothed me; sick, and ye visited me. I was in prison, and ye came to me," (Matthew 25:35, 40). From here you are to learn how acceptable such works as these are, and you should be stirred up to abound in them. But other works are not excluded, for afterwards our Lord only mentions the mercilessness and uncharitable omissions of the wicked, and yet it is plain from other Scriptures, that their other sins will be punished such as their not knowing God, and their "disobedience to the Gospel of Christ," (2 Thessalonians 1:8).

3. The sentence which will be passed on them will be a sentence of absolution. They shall be absolved and acquitted openly before men and angels. All their sins will be forgotten and buried. There will be an eternal deliverance from the curse. With what admiration, joy, and triumph will they hear, "Come ye blessed of my Father, inherit the kingdom prepared for you, from the foundation of the world," (Matthew 25:34). What a kingdom that is, that shall never be moved! What a crown that is, that is incorruptible! What gladness will fill their hearts, when the crown of life is put on their heads! The sentence being pronounced, presently it will be done according to this sentence. Possession will be taken of the glorious inheritance, they shall "enter into eternal life," (Matthew 25:46). So much of the righteous.

Chapter 5: Things to be Judged

I am to also speak concerning the wicked, and as to these, you must understand:

1. All the works of wicked men will be brought into judgment. All their sinful deeds will follow them to the bar of God! They will rise with them, and against them at that day, when a sinner shall appear, and all his drunkenness, his whoredoms, his unjust and cheating actions, all his evil deeds of every sort, shall surround and appear with him, before the holy and righteous judge! How will he be amazed at the sight of all his transgressions! How will he tremble to hear how loud they cry for vengeance on him! All deeds of darkness will then be brought to light, to his greater confusion!

2. Not only the works of the wicked, but their very words shall be accounted for. The Judge himself speaks this very plainly, "But I say unto you, that every idle word that men shall speak, they shall give an account thereof in the day of judgment," (Matthew 12:36). By *idle words* may be meant words useless and unprofitable to the speakers and to the hearers; or idle and vain, according to the Hebrew use, may signify false, deceitful, lying. God hears all words at present, "There is not a word in my tongue, but lo, O Lord, thou knowest it altogether," (Psalm 139:4). And words which declare very much what most abounds in the heart, must be answered for at last. And if unprofitable talk will then be

condemned, how sad will be the case of all obscene and filthy speakers, egregious liars, injurious slanderers and backbiters, blasphemers, and cursing cursed swearers! Of all whose impious tongues have made bold with the blood and wounds of God their Judge, and instead of serious praying, have most presumptuously called on, and dared God to damn them!

3. As the works and words, so the thoughts of the wicked men shall be brought into judgment. Thoughts are sins, and need forgiveness, and ought to be repented of. What Simon Peter says to Simon Magus is memorable, "Repent therefore of this thy wickedness, and pray God, if perhaps the thought of thy heart may be forgiven thee," (Acts 8:22). If these are not repented of and pardoned, alas, these also must be charged on sinners vastly to the increasing of their punishment. How innumerable are the thousands of thousands, the millions of millions of vain and wicked thoughts, desires and lusts that have lodged their way into the hearts of the ungodly! The heart searcher sees every one of them, and will make them know at the last day, that he remembers all. Proud and self-conceited thoughts, and touring imaginations; impure and lascivious thoughts, and inward boiling of concupiscence; insatiable covetousness, and eager projects for filthy gain; the stirrings of envy, malice anger, and revenge. The Judge will take notice of all; for "he knows what

is in man," (John 2:25). It will be a large bill of indictment, where deeds, words, and thoughts are all written down from the first to the last, and not so much as one forgotten. The opening of the book of God's remembrance, where all are recorded, will be very amazing.

4. The sentence that will be passed on the wicked will be inconceivably full of horror. "Then shall he say to them on the left hand, depart from me ye cursed into everlasting fire, prepared for the devil and his angels," (Matthew 25:41). For him, who is the way to come to God, to say "Depart!" to depart from Christ, the sinner's only hope and Savior, to depart with a curse, to depart into fire, the extremity of torment, to depart into everlasting fire, to be tormented without any intermission or end! To be in such evil and hateful company, as devils and damned angels! This is woeful beyond all utterance! And this sentence, as soon as it is passed, will be put in execution. Now indeed, such is the patience of God. Sentence against an evil work is not speedily executed, and therefore such is their malignity and ingratitude, "the heart of the sons of men is fully set in them to do evil," (Ecclesiastes 8:11). But at the great day, as soon as the wicked are sentenced, they will be sent, and forced to go away into everlasting punishment, (Matthew 25:46). The words εἰς κόλασιν αἰώνιον, everlasting punishment or torment, are

remarkable, for here it is necessarily implied, that the wicked shall certainly exist to eternity, that they may be punished and tormented to eternity; and they shall be sensible (or else it would not be torment) of the punishment they undergo. By eternal destruction, you are not to understand eternal annihilation, or being turned forever into nothing. For if a wicked man should altogether cease to exist, he will also cease to be punished. For it is no more a punishment to be nothing to eternity, than it can be called a punishment to have been nothing from eternity. Wicked men must exist forever, and alas they must forever bear the Lord's vengeance and indignation. I speak xo terribly, not without bowels of compassion towards you. I would gladly frighten you by telling you of wrath, and the vengeance of eternal fire, that you may never, never feel it.

CHAPTER 6:
THE CERTAINTY OF JUDGMENT

In the fourth place, I am to demonstrate the certainty of this judgment. If faith concerning it were only more strong, what an influence it would have on the hearts and lives of those that believe it! The arguments to prove a future judgment are *these*:

1. Are there not fears of this judgment impressed even on natural conscience? What is the reason, that when men commit the most secret wickedness, that is very unlikely to be known, there is notwithstanding a dread on their spirits? The true reason is, conscience tells them there is a God, that sees what man does not see, and that he will judge and punish the wickedness of which man takes no notice. This doctrine of a judgment to come, or future rewards and punishments, is written in the heart of man by nature, and he is glad to offer great violence to his own soul before he can wear off what is written there. And though a sinner may become ordinarily very stupid and atheistic, yet the thoughts and fears of judgment will sometimes return to him, in spite of him. The apostle speaks of "conscience bearing witness, and thoughts accusing and excusing;" and then presently "speaks of the day

when God shall judge the secrets of men by Jesus Christ," (Romans 2:15-16). Conscience judges at present, and hints at a future judgment.

2. There is not such a discrimination made in this world between the righteous and the wicked, as is suitable to the difference that grace has made between them. Therefore, there is a day coming, when there will be such a discrimination. Solomon tells us that in the course of divining providence at present, "no man can know either love or hatred by all that is before him. All things fall alike to all. There is one event to the righteous and to the wicked, to the good, to the clean, and to the unclean; to him that sacrificeth, and him that sacrificeth not; as is the good, so is the sinner. and he that sweareth, as he that feareth an oath," (Ecclesiastes 9:1-2). No, often times the worst of men have the best in this present life. In Luke 16, we read of a wicked rich man receiving his good things, clothed in purple and fine linen, and faring sumptuously every day. A poor man ready to starve on account of hunger was laid at this rich man's gate, his body was full of sores, and yet this man's soul was sanctified with grace. He was a good man, though he received evil things. Since it is this way now, there is a day coming when it will be otherwise. Job, having spoken of the prosperity of the wicked in this world, strongly argues that in the next world there will

Chapter 6: The Certainty of Judgment

be a dreadful after-reckoning. "The wicked is reserved to the day of destruction, they shall be brought forth to the day of wrath," (Job 21:30). This is the day I am speaking of, a day in revelation of the righteous judgment of God. "Who then will render to every man according to his works, to them that by patient continuance in well doing seek for glory, and honor, and immortality, eternal life. but to them that are contentious, and do not obey the truth, but obey unrighteousness, indignation and wrath, tribulation and anguish on every soul of man that doeth evil, of the Jew first, and also of the gentile," (Romans 2:5-9).

    3. Christ has promised his church that he will come again to judgment, and has raised her hopes and expectations of his coming. "Behold I come quickly, hold that fast which thou hast, that none make take thy crown," (Revelation 3:11). "For yet a little while, and he that shall come, will come, and will not tarry," (Hebrews 10:36). He speaks to his disciples in this way, "Let not your hearts be troubled, ye believe in God, believe also in me;" I am indeed about to leave you, but "I go to prepare a place for you;" and assure yourselves, "I will come again, and receive you to myself, that where I am, there ye may be also," (John 14:1-5). Christ is the *Amen*, the true and faithful Witness, he will certainly be the Judge. The church will assuredly see him at last on the great white throne, and herself

safe and triumphant at his right hand. When he comes, how will he be glorified in his saints, and how will he be "admired by all believers in that day!" (2 Thessalonians 1:10).

4. There are several things that are hastening Christ's coming to judgment. The world grows old in wickedness, and all the sins of the world have tongues to cry for the appearing of a Judge, to pay their deserved wages. The world grows riper and riper for vengeance, drier and drier for the fire that is to burn it. The church of Christ is also hastening Christ's appearing, with their incessant cries, "Come Lord Jesus, come quickly." "The Spirit and the bride say, Come," (Revelation 22:20). Not only is this said to sinners to come to Christ, but to Christ himself to appear, that he may put an end to both sin and suffering. That is the longing and language of the spouse, "Make haste, my Beloved, and be like a roe, or a young hart on the mountains of spices," (Song of Solomon 8:14). And this is not only the voice of the church on earth, but they in heaven wish for and entreat the same thing. "How long, Lord, holy and true!" is heard from the "Souls under the Altar," (Revelation 6:10).

CHAPTER 7:
APPLICATION OF THE WARNING

In the last place, I come to the application. I begin with the inferences from the *doctrine*:

1. If there will be a day of judgment, here I infer, that there is a present providence. Will the Lord judge all at last? Surely he observes all now. The Lord Jesus would have all the churches to know as well, that he searches the reins and heart, and that he will "render to every man according to his works," (Revelation 2:23). Whether your eye is on God or not, his eye is never off of you. It is in every place, beholding the evil and the good. What a foolish creature do you have reason to call yourself, who "considers not in thy heart that God remembers all thy wickedness," (Hosea 7:2) and God's remembrance at last will press yours, and what you now forget, will sadly be recalled to your mind.

2. Shall all be judged? Here I infer the love of God to the righteous, and his hatred of iniquity. Not one righteous man, but shall be acquitted and received by the Judge. Not a righteous action, or sincere intention, but shall be rewarded. It will be found at the last day that a widow's mite given with a charitable spirit, and according to the ability, was a great

deal in God's treasury, and that a cup of cold water given to a disciple, in the name of a disciple, was well taken, and shall not go unrewarded, (Matthew 10:42). And there has not been, there is not a wicked man on earth, but his sin that has been hunting and pursuing to overthrow him, will then find him out, (Psalm 11:5-6) because the Lord's soul hates the workers of iniquity. Therefore on "the wicked he will rain snares, fire and brimstone, and an horrible tempest, this shall be the portion of their cup." By fire, and brimstone, and tempest, understand a sudden, grievous, surprising and intolerable punishment, and by snares understand, that those in hell shall never be able to extricate themselves out of that misery into which their wickedness has brought them.

3. If all shall be judged, here I infer the truth of the doctrine of the resurrection. The whole man has sinned, the whole man shall be judged and punished for sin. Believers are sanctified both in soul and body, therefore in body and soul they shall be glorified. The dead shall rise again, all that are "in the graves shall hear the voice of Christ, and shall come forth. They that have done good to the resurrection of life, they that have done evil to the resurrection of damnation," (John 5:28-29). The grave is only a prison for a time, not a body that is there shall always lie there. The same body that was employed in the unfruitful works of darkness, shall be raised by the

Chapter 7: The Application of the Warning

power of the righteous Judge, to share in the demerited punishment. And the same body of the saints, the members of which were used as instruments of righteousness to holiness, by virtue of its union with Christ, shall rise again, and be "made like unto Christ's glorious body, according to the working whereby he is able to subdue all things to himself," (Philippians 3:21). It is not another body. I grant that qualities are altered, but the substance is the same, therefore the apostle does not stick to say τὸ φθαρτὸν το θανατὸν τατο. "This corruptible shall put on incorruption, this mortal shall put on immorality. So when this corruptible shall have put on incorruption, and this mortal shall have put on immortality, then shall be brought to pass the saying that is written, death is swallowed up in victory," (1 Corinthians 15:53-54).

    4. Will there be a judgment, it is wonderful that there should be so much security in those that hear of it. Really, the very mention of Christ's tribunal, before which all must stand, should make all criminals to tremble. If a man was seized for a crime that is capital, deserving death by the law of God and man, and being in bolts and fetters in Newgate, if he was secure and unconcerned, though the *Sessious* were at hand, you would conclude him to be very stupid and inconsiderate. What, sinner, secure! And shortly to be judged! O drunkard! Whoremonger! Swearer! Sabbath-breaker! Covetous

worldling! They will secure and speedily appear at the judgment seat of Christ, who has said, that those who do such things, shall not inherit the kingdom of God! Sin is folly, security in sin is the folly of that folly. Take heed of security, Christ himself also gives you this necessary caution, "And take heed to yourselves, lest at any time your hearts be overcharged with surfeiting and drunkenness, and the cares of this life, and so that day come on you unawares. For as a snare shall come on all them that dwell on the face of the whole earth. Watch ye therefore, and pray always, that ye may be accounted worthy to escape all those things that shall come to pass, and to stand before the Son of Man," (Luke 21:34-36).

Use 2, by way of counsel. I would give two words of counsel to this congregation.

First, believe a judgment more firmly, and think of it more frequently.

Second, be sure to prepare in time for eternal judgment.

1. More firmly believe, more frequently think of judgment. You have reason to believe it, for the Judge is ordained, and though neither men nor angels know the day, yet the day is appointed. "The time of this ignorance God winked at, but now commands all men everywhere to repent, because he hath appointed a day in which he will judge the

Chapter 7: The Application of the Warning

world in righteousness, by that Man whom he hath ordained. whereof he hath given assurance to all, in that he hath raised him from the dead," (Acts 17:30-31). The stronger your assent is to this, the more serious and often your consideration of it will be.

To think of judgment is proper for a saint, that he may be encouraged to fight the good fight of faith, and persevere in well doing to the end.

To think of judgment is proper for a wicked man, to awaken him, and to make him work out his salvation with fear and trembling.

It is proper for a hypocrite to think of judgment, because then all masks and visors will be pulled off, all shows will be at an end, and naked truth will appear at that day. The graves will be opened, and do you think the white washed sepulchers will remain shut? O! then all the conceited pride, filthiness, selfishness, sensuality, injustice, and earthliness of professors will with all their aggravations be brought to light before men and angels. O! how many demure and serious countenances, that have been a covering to naughty hearts, will then be filled with confusion!

It is proper for the old to think of judgment. They have one foot in the grace already, and quickly the whole body must drop into it, and the spirit must return to God who gave it. You also that are young should think of judgment, have the youngest of you any assurance of your lives? Infants, children, youths, do not many of them die and step into eternity? And as you see them leave the world, so certainly they appear before God, and one way or another have their doom. Solomon tells you that childhood and youth are vanity. Would you that are young be serious? The meditation of judgment would conduce much to it, "Rejoice, O young man, in thy youth, and let thy heart cheer thee in the days of thy youth, and walk in the ways of thy heart, and in the sight of thine eyes," (Ecclesiastes 11:9). He says, rejoice, while taken with things that are seen, and while you walk in those evil ways which your heart naturally likes. Then the wise man speaks seriously, "But know thou, that for all these things God will bring thee to judgment."

If you ask me, what are the benefits that will accrue by a firm belief, and frequent meditation of judgment? I answer this way to this momentous question:

1. This will be a great preservation against temptation. Look beyond the present advantage and delight that sin boasts of, and see as far as the judgment seat, this is the way to silence the tempter, and to avoid his snare. Would the liar dare to speak falsely, if he considered that all liars shall be judged to "the lake that burns with fire and brimstone, which

is the second death?" (Revelation 21:8). Would the unclean person dare to defile himself, and run to the harlot's house, if he believed and considered that God will judge whoremongers and adulterers? Improve Christ's cross, and think of Christ's tribunal, and this will cool and kill corruptions, and take away the force of your temptations.

2. The belief and meditation of judgment will cause you to use this world as not abusing it, to make a good improvement of it. You that have this world in great abundance, and have the clearest and largest estates. Do you think you are proprietors of what you have? Do you think it is given or only lent to you for a time? You are only stewards of God's and not yours, and are accountable at the last day for all you have received. What sad accounts will most give up of their stewardship. When they must no longer be stewards! *Imprimis*, so much daily for eating and drinking to self, and not to the glory of God. *Item*, so much for brave apparel, that pride might be maintained and gratified. *Item*, so much for making provision for the flesh, to fulfill the lusts of it. *Item*, so much for costly and vast past-times. a great deal of wealth, and much more precious time being wasted together. But to good uses, to maintain a godly and laborious ministry of the Gospel, to the poor and needy, given very little or nothing. With what an eye do you think that the Judge will look on such accounts

as these? Think of judgment that you may holily improve the unrighteous mammon, and Christ may say you have been faithful stewards, even of worldly things.

3. The belief and meditation of judgment will make you exceedingly diligent, that you may be found of your Judge in peace, without spot and blameless. With what seriousness and fervency will he come to the throne of grace, that has the judgment seat also in his eye? How will he hear and practice, that remembers he must be called to an account, how he has done both? He will take care to be ready whenever the Lord calls, and that whenever his Lord comes, he may find him doing the work he set him about, and so doing it as he commands.

2. The other word of counsel is this, be sure to prepare in time for eternal judgment. Do this seriously, do it presently, and as your main business, that you may prepare indeed.

1. Be accusers and judges of yourselves. Take notice of your sins, with grief, with hatred, and holy indignation! Accuse yourselves of them before God, with self-loathing and self-abhorrence. Look down by faith into the lowest hell, and see the terrible but righteous severity that is shown there against obstinate workers of iniquity. Then look up to God, and judge yourselves in his sight, acknowledging that you have deserved one of the hottest places in that lake of fire.

Chapter 7: The Application of the Warning

Acknowledge that God would be clear in the sorest judgment he should pronounce on you, and that he would be justified, though you should be damned eternally, (Psalm 51:4). This judging of yourselves is the way to prevent condemnation with the world, (1 Corinthians 11:31-32).

2. If you would be prepared for judgment, believe in Jesus, that you may be justified before God, at present. Receive Christ, who is offered in the Gospel. Rely on his obedience and sufferings for justification of life. And being justified by faith, you shall "have peace with God through our Lord Jesus Christ," (Romans 5:1). "Being justified by his blood, you shall be saved from wrath through him, (Romans 5:9).

What does *ponere obicem* (*set up an obstacle*), put a bar before hell's gate, and hinder us from falling into that place of woe? The cross of Christ, that is the bar. You are to place your confidence in Christ crucified. If justified by him now, he will ratify the justification at the last day, and you shall not be condemned then. "Who shall lay anything to the charge of God's elect? It is God that justifieth. Who is he that condemneth? It is Christ that died, yea, rather that is risen again. who is at the right hand of God, and maketh intercession for us," (Romans 8:33-34).

3. Would you be prepared for judgment? Repent and be converted. Let your minds be changed and turn to God

with your whole heart. This is the way indeed to stand before him. "Repent and be converted, that your sins may be blotted out, when the times of refreshing shall come from the presence of the Lord," (Acts 3:19). The apostle looks as far as the last day. Blotting out sins, is Christ's absolving and acquitting them from all trespasses. The time of refreshing, is that great day of complete and glorious redemption, when all that are Christ's shall lift up their heads with joy. Repent and be converts in truth, if you would have that to be a day of refreshing, and not of confusion. Walk after the flesh no longer, but after the Spirit. Then you need not be afraid of condemnation, your being guided by his Spirit will show that you are in Christ, and safe in Him. "There is therefore now no condemnation to them that are in Christ Jesus, who walk not after the flesh, but after the Spirit. to be carnally minded is death, but to be spiritually minded is life and peace," (Romans 8:1).

Use 3, of terror to the ungodly, the hypocrites, and the unbelievers. Christ will judge them all, and they may tremble to think what kind of judgment they shall have. What sharp and piercing words are those, which declare beforehand what will be their doom. "Ye serpents, ye generation of vipers, how can ye escape the damnation of hell?" (Matthew 23:33). That I

Chapter 7: The Application of the Warning

may, if possible, awaken such, I would lay before them these terrifying considerations.

    1. When they appear at Christ's bar, all their secret wickedness will be made known. How many will then be found to be what they were not in the least expected to be! Your secret wantonness, and self-pollutions. Your secret injustice and defrauding. Your secret abominations of all kinds, will then be visible to every eye, as if written in capital letters with the brightest sunbeam. And what shame and confusion will cover the wicked man's face! Those that are imprudent and cannot blush now. How they will be confounded then! The truth is, as the prophet Daniel speaks. "They will rise to shame and everlasting contempt," (Daniel 12:2).

    2. At the Day of Judgment it will be too late, and also vain for the wicked to pray and cry for mercy. They will find the Lord eternally removed from the throne of grace, and to their terror, behold him on the judgment seat. If the ungodly roar out then, "Lord pity! Lord pardon! Lord, send us not away into that flaming furnace that we see before us!" It will be altogether in vain. But it is not in vain to cry out now. "Oh, seek the Lord while he may be found, and call ye on him whilst he is near," (Isaiah 55:6).

3. It will add to the terror of the wicked, that the sentence of condemnation is pronounced by the only Savior. The merciful and faithful High Priest, that now is so forward to make reconciliation for sin, that is so ready to give rest to those that labor and are heavy laden. The man Christ Jesus will have no pity at all, no compassion towards the reprobate children of men. But he will deal with them as with the apostate angels, whose nature he never took on himself. The only peacemaker will himself be so incensed and full of wrath, as not to be entreated, and not to be appeased. The sentence of eternal death, and enduring, everlasting burdens, will be confounding. But it will add to the confusion, that a Redeemer pronounces it.

4. After the Judge has passed the sentence, conscience will pronounce it over again, and will be a judge to the wicked, always condemning them. Conscience will be filled with unspeakable remorse. It will continually be upbraiding them with their madness and folly in keeping their sins, and losing their souls. And will ever be telling them, that "the Lord's ways towards them are equal, but their own ways according to which they are judged, have been unequal," and full of iniquity, (Ezekiel 18:29-30). The conscience of sinners will side with their Judge against them. It will tell the most wretched among the damned, that they cannot complain of

Chapter 7: The Application of the Warning

God, or of the least injury that he has done to them. All that they suffer, they suffer justly. and what they suffer, they have brought on themselves. The horrible and perpetual remorse of conscience, will prove that the worm that torments them will never die.

    5. When sinners come to be condemned at the last day, how many things will rise up in judgment against them? Thousands of mercies will come, and as it were plead this way against them. "Lord, we have been all abused, we never met with anything but abuses, and never could lead these men to repentance!" The rods of affliction will have a voice against them too. "Lord, we have stricken these sinners often, we have made them bleed and groan, and hurt exceedingly for their iniquities, but could never make them leave off sinning against Thee, and against their own souls!" How many sermons will rise up in judgment against them, because they either slept them away. Or if they were awake, they suffered them to slip out of their memories, and never applied them to their hearts! And as for us, the ministers of the Gospel, our testimony against them will be true and terrible. "Lord, we lifted up our voices like trumpets. We gave them the watchman's warning, we told them of the sword that was coming, and that if they turned not from sin, it would surely slay them. We wooed them to come to Jesus, that under his wing they might be

secure, but nothing would prevail. Their ears were deaf, their hearts they hardened, they would not be converted and made clean, they would rush on in sin still, they would necessarily die, and there was no helping it!" The condemnation must necessarily be dreadful, when so many things rise up against those that are condemned!

Use 4, of consolation to the saints. I must speak to them in another strain. Lift up your heads, and let your hearts be filled with joy, all you believing, repenting, humble, holy, heavenly-minded ones, for the day of your redemption draws near! Wait for it with an earnest expectation, and triumph at the thoughts of your great and everlasting jubilee. You will indeed behold the greatest part of mankind turned into hell. But what joy it will be to find yourselves forever safe and fully blessed! A dark shadow sets off a beautiful picture. The sight of the rich man in hell's flames must necessarily make Lazarus to find a greater sweetness in Abraham's bosom!

I shall propound two grounds of consolation to you, and so conclude this *chapter:*

1. He is to be your Judge, that is your Husband and your Head. The very same whom you now find interceding for you in prayer whom you see walking in the midst of the golden candlesticks, and blessing his ordinances to you. The very same whom you have found pitying, and healing your

Chapter 7: The Application of the Warning

wounds with his own blood, succoring you in your temptations, and telling you that you are the beloved of his soul! And since his is to judge you, be comforted. He will behold you with an aspect that is highly favorable! His own spouse, whom he has ransomed with his own life, Christ will not turn into a devouring fire! He will not take the members of his own body, and throw them into everlasting burnings! Having redeemed them by his blood, having renewed and sanctified them by his Spirit. having raised them up at the great day. certainly he will receive them to himself, and they shall be "ever with the Lord, wherefore be comforted with these words," (1 Thessalonians 4:17-18).

2. You that are true believers, whose faith purifies your hearts and works by love. Know that there is a crown designed for you. The diadems that monarchs have on their heads, the triple crown of he who is in Rome, is but a trifle to the crown of life. This crown is purchased, it is promised, it is prepared. And shortly you shall put it on, and never take it off again. How splendid, how bright, how sparkling, will that crown be! It is called a crown of life, for death shall be no more. A crown of glory, for the saints shall be more than conquerors, and triumphant over all enemies, and be advanced to the highest honor and state, whereof they are capable. Finally, it is called a crown of righteousness. It is a righteous

thing with God, to bestow it through Christ Jesus, and perfect righteousness and purity will be a great part of the happiness of saints in glory. The apostle saw this crown, to his great encouragement, and he would have all other believers comforted with the same sight. "I have fought the good fight, I have finished my course, I have kept the faith. From here forth there is laid up for me a crown of righteousness, which the Lord, the Righteous Judge shall give me at that day, and not to me only, "but unto all them also that love his appearing," (2 Timothy 4:7-8).

CHAPTER 8:
THE DAMNATION OF HELL

"And thou Capernaum, which are exalted unto heaven, shalt be brought down to hell!" (Matthew 11:23).

Our Lord Jesus is called *the Lamb of God, who takes away the sin of the world*. But in this Lamb there is wrath, and that wrath is very terrible. O! the weight of the Mediators vengeance! This wrath is threatened against the impenitent and unbelievers, who refuse to be saved from their sins, resolving to live, though they die in them. The light of the Gospel, being neglected, highly aggravates the works of darkness. It makes them more inexcusable, and a greater provocation. None shall fare worse at the Day of Judgment, than those that have had the longest and the clearest day of grace, but would not know in their day, the things which belonged to their peace. "Thou Capernaum which art exalted unto heaven, shalt be brought down to hell."

These words of the text speak of Christ's sorrow and his displeasure, in which you make take *notice*:

1. Of the people with whom he is displeased, "Thou Capernaum;" the city is stated for the inhabitants of it.

2. Here is the reason of Christ's displeasure. They did not understand the great privilege of being exalted to heaven. They did not improve the advantage they had of getting there.

3. Here is a punishment threatened, a sore evil, and that is no less than hell itself.

4. Here is the manner specified of their going to hell, "Thou shalt be brought down to hell," with a strong hand, with great wrath, and in one of the hottest and lowest places, you shall lie forever.

There are two doctrines which I raise from the words.

DOCTRINE 1: First, those that hear the Gospel, are exalted to heaven. Happy are you, if you understand your privilege which you enjoy on this day.

DOCTRINE 2: Secondly, "They who will not turn to God at the Gospel call shall certainly be turned into hell. Thou Capernaum, who art exalted unto heaven, shalt be brought down to hell;" and if Christ says it shall be so, most certainly it will be so. I shall only touch on the first of these, for it is the second that I principally purpose to prosecute.

Doctrine 1. Those that hear the Gospel are exalted to heaven. The Gospel is a heavenly calling, (Hebrews 3:1) and it comes from heaven, and says to those that hear it, "Come up hither."

Chapter 8: The Damnation of Hell

1. Life and immortality is brought to light by the Gospel, (2 Timothy 1:10). Here you have a map of those happy regions of light, love, and joy, where there is nothing present that is burdensome, where there is nothing wanting that is desirable.

2. The Gospel plainly chalks out the way that leads to life. Christ is the way, the truth, and the life, (John 14:6) the true way to life indeed. We have liberty to enter into the holiest of all, by the blood of Jesus. Had it not been for his undertaking and performance of what he undertook, there had been a flaming sword at heaven's gate, and no fallen man could ever have entered there. And as Christ, in whom we are to believe, is the way, so also is holiness. Christ, by his blood has purchased the heavenly inheritance, and has bought the saints themselves that are to be the inheritors, and it is by his sanctifying Spirit, by true holiness, that they are made fit for that inheritance. The pure in heart, and those who will be likewise pure in life, are the blessed ones that shall see God, (Matthew 5:8), and who besides are desirous or fit to see the Lord?

3. Heaven is offered in the Gospel. It is seriously, freely offered to all. It is offered to the meanest people, it is offered to the greatest sinners, and that without money, without price. It is indeed too good, too great a thing for man to purchase by

anything that he can give or do. Those have very low thoughts of heaven, and very high thoughts of their own works, that think they can do enough to merit heaven. Eternal life is the free gift of God, not deserved by man. And it is given through Christ, (Romans 6:23). If Christ had not procured it, fallen men would all have been as certainly excluded as the fallen angels.

Briefly to apply this:

1. Be thankful for the Gospel, which makes the richest discovery that ever was made in this world. The East, the West Indies cannot show anything comparable to a blessed immortality. The jewels from this one, the gold from the other, are contemptible when heaven is named. The Gospel tells you where to find the true, tried gold, and the Pearl that is of greatest price. and concerning "treasure in heaven, which neither moth nor rust doth corrupt, nor can thieves break through and steal," (Matthew 6:20).

2. Let the kingdom of heaven suffer violence, and use a holy force to take it. Here you will meet with great opposition. Heaven is that which occasions the envy of hell, because of its real and eternal excellence, and does very well deserve your labor. Let the treasure in heaven cause your hearts to be there, strive to enter in at the strait gate, hate every false way, because it leads from heaven, and towards

Chapter 8: The Damnation of Hell

destruction. Let the hopes of a crown of glory make you willing to bear the cross. Look on sloth as most absurd, when no less than heaven will be given to those who show their diligence in full assurance of hope to the end. Press still forward towards the mark. You cannot run too fast for such a prize. But I shall stay on this no longer. It is the second doctrine that I shall more largely insist on.

CHAPTER 9:
TURN TO GOD
OR TURN INTO HELL

Doctrine 2. Those that will not turn to God at the call of the Gospel, shall certainly be turned into hell. "They that know not God, and that obey not the Gospel of our Lord Jesus Christ, shall be punished with everlasting destruction from the presence of the Lord, and from the glory of his power," (2 Thessalonians 1:8-9).

In the handling of this doctrine, I shall:

1. Discourse concerning hell, what it is, that you may better understand it. and understanding it, be afraid of it.

2. I shall prove the certainty of the doctrine that sinners who will not turn to God, shall most surely be turned into hell.

3. I shall vindicate the righteousness of God, in thus dealing with, and eternally punishing those that will not turn to him.

4. I shall conclude with the uses and application.

In the first place I am to discourse concerning hell, and to show you what it is. In *hell*:

Chapter 9: Turn to God or Turn into Hell

There is a deprivation of good.

There is an infliction of evil, pains and torment.

There is an eternity of both.

1. In hell there is a deprivation of good. All the temporal losses that have been sustained by all the children of men in this world, are not comparable to the *Poena Damni*, punishment of loss, which one sinner in hell shall undergo. Those in hell are deprived of several things:

1. They are deprived of all that love and grace, and mercy that is in God. The psalmist knew by experience the excellence of God's loving kindness, and affirms that it is better than life, (Psalm 63:3). His mercies are tender, and a multitude, and sure to the vessels of mercy. How were those filled with admiration, and with a sense of their obligation, "Who in times past were not a people, but were made the people of God, who had not obtained mercy, but after did obtain mercy," (1 Peter 2:10). But alas, though God is love itself, (1 John 4:8) he has no love for those that are in hell, they lie under his wrath and hatred, and both are unalterably fixed on them. Though the Lord delights in showing mercy, yet his bowels do not stir at all or move towards the damned. Though they lie in extreme woe, and are continually weeping and wailing, yet their tears do not draw forth his compassions. He has cast them off forever, and will be favorable no more. He

has forgotten to be gracious, and implacable, but righteous anger, has shut up his tender mercies.

2. Those that are in hell are deprived of the beatifical vision of God. The door of heaven has been shut against them, when they said, "Lord, Lord open to us!" and it will never be opened. They shall never be suffered to see him face to face, but always will be excluded from his presence. What happiness there is in seeing God! How transforming and satisfying is this sight! "As for me, I shall behold thy face in righteousness, I shall be satisfied when I awake with thy likeness," (Psalm 17:15). But the damned are not, and never shall be admitted to such a view. They are banished from the glorious presence, where there is fullness of joy, and where there are pleasures forevermore. God has fixed a great gulf between himself and them, and through that it is impossible for them to pass, (Luke 16:26).

3. Those in hell are deprived of all hopes by a Mediator. Our Lord tells us that he came "not into the world to condemn the world, but that the world through him might be saved;" and has given a large commission to preach the Gospel, to offer that grace and salvation of which he is the Author, to every creature, (Mark 16:15). The Lord Jesus now encourages all to come to him, that they have rest to their souls, and life through his Name, and "them that come to him, he will in no

wise cast out," (John 6:37) and when they refuse to come, he expresses great sorrow. He wept over Jerusalem, because she did not know the time of her visitation. But when sinners have sinned away the day of grace, and ended all their days on earth, and by their final impenitence, brought themselves to hell then the same chains are clapped on them, in which the reprobate angels lie fettered, and Christ will no more save them than these. O! how dreadful to lose all hope in Jesus, never to be called to come to him again. Astonishingly fearful to be in the place where the glad tidings of the Gospel are never heard, where the Spirit never strives, and where the Redeemer never stretches forth a hand to save!

4. Those in hell are deprived of the glory of the New Jerusalem. It is a mighty loss, to lose such a "weighty thing as a far more exceeding and eternal weight of glory," (2 Corinthians 4:17). Suppose a rich man, worth millions, should become poor, and not be worth a farthing. Suppose all the kings and emperors breathing, should lose their crowns in one day, this would be a petty loss, compared with the loss of a crown of life. In heaven there is such a crown, and the damned might have had it, if they had valued it. But alas, they must never wear that crown. In heaven there is a kingdom where those in hell must never reign. When they see what they have lost, and how foolishly, willfully, and for the sake of what

poor things they lost it, how will they be filled with heart tearing vexation, and be quite overwhelmed with sorrow. "There shall be weeping and gnashing of teeth. When ye shall see Abraham, and Isaac, and Jacob, and all the prophets, in the kingdom of heaven, and you yourselves thrust out."

1. As in hell there is a deprivation of good, so there is an infliction of evil, pain and torment.

1.) There is great torment in the conscience in hell. A wounded conscience in this world has been found intolerable. *Spira*, he signifies that racks, gibbets, flames of martyrdom, were nothing to what he felt, and in a pang of despair attempts suicide. But being hindered, he breaks out into blasphemy, "I wish I were above God, for I know he will not have mercy on me:" here was hells language in his mouth, and much of hell's torment in his heart. Judas' conscience was wounded, and could he bear it? No, he becomes his own executioner, with his own hand he ends his life, and sends his soul to his appointed place. And yet the torment of conscience in this world, is but the *Praludium*, the beginning of sorrows. Every conscience in hell will be thoroughly awake, and keep itself forever waking. It will be exactly sensible. Every sin that has been committed in all the lifetime will have made a wound in the conscience. And all these wounds will be intolerably smarting, without hope of any ease. Conscience will be in perpetual agony, in this agony it will rage, and raging it will reproach the damned. It will tell them of their presumptuous sinning, of their rejecting Christ, their neglecting great salvation, and how all its checking of them was in vain. And now it is incurably wounded, and can never be quiet, but that shall always find it to be a tormenting fury within them.

2.) There is in hell, not only torment in the conscience, but also torment in the mind and heart. What woeful thoughts will possess their minds! Whatever they think of will be torturing. a pleasing, a delightful thought can never enter into them again. If they think of sin, it will be bitter to consider how they have been deceived and ruined by it. If they think of their present misery, and how it is without remedy, and that they themselves had the greatest hand in bringing themselves to it, these thoughts will pierce their souls like daggers. If they think of God, O! how will they be troubled! How will this justice, jealousy, fury, holiness, truth, irresistible power, and unchangeableness terrify them! Thoughts on earth were their sins, and thoughts in hell will be their racks and sorrows. Their hearts will always be full to the brim with grief. Shame and confusion of face will add to their misery, when all their wickedness shall be known to all, which will make the justness of their punishment evident. And how will they be tormented with anger at the very heart, and indignation against themselves because, though the devil was their great enemy, yet they themselves were far greater enemies to themselves than he was.

3.) There will be torment in sinner's memories in hell. I wish that none of you that hear me this day, may in that place of woe, remember this day, may in that place of woe, remember the warning now given to you, to your confusion, because you would not take it. Listen at what was said, "Son, remember thou in thy lifetime received thy good things, and Lazarus evil things. But he is comforted, and thou art tormented," (Luke 16:25). Really the remembrance of what he had, what he was, and what he did on earth, was very tormenting to this wretched rich man in hell. The damned there will remember their delicious fare, and how sensual and brutish they were in pleasing their appetites. They will remember the time they spent in adorning themselves, taking many pains to dress and trick the carcass, but no pains at all to purge the heart. They will remember their feasts, their mirth, their carnal jollity, which quite stupefied their hearts, and banished all thoughts and cares about another world and eternity. They will remember all the mercies they enjoyed, which they did nothing but abuse to their own harm, as well as to the dishonor of God who gave them.

Above all, they will remember what pains were taken to have prevented their destruction. The Lord was unwilling that they should perish, but death was preferred before life by them. O! how long did Christ come, Sabbath after Sabbath, and knock at the door, but they would not open! How often did the Spirit strive with them, to stop them in hell's road, and to turn them into the way of peace, but they were stiff-necked, and always resisted the Holy Spirit. They will remember their preacher's pains and prayers, and labors and travail of soul. How they lifted up their voices, to awaken them out of their sin and security. How they entreated them to be reconciled to God, and to turn into the safe and blessed paths of righteousness. But they were deaf and obstinate, nothing would prevail with them, and the remembrance of all this will be bitter, bitter, bitter to them.

2. In hell there will be torment in the body and the members of it, and such as nobody ever felt, or was capable of bearing here on earth. The stone, the colic, and the strangery, the greatest torture that the hand of man ever inflicted, are no more comparable to the pains of hell, than the smallest prick of a pin is to a dagger that strikes through, and gives the heart a deadly wound. The senses of the damned shall have that which will be exceedingly afflicting. What woeful spectacles their eyes will behold! What dismal noises will fill their ears!

How fierce and unquenchable are the flames that they shall feel! All their parts shall be in pain, not so much as one free. The whole body was defiled, and at sin's service, all the members were yielded as members of unrighteousness. It is only righteous that all should be punished. Why are the bodies of the wicked raised at the last day? Surely that they may bear their part in the condemnation, which the whole man by sin has deserved. This resurrection is certain, but it is a dreadful resurrection, which is a "resurrection to damnation," (John 5:29).

In these torments you may well suppose that death will be wished for, and that the damned would rejoice if they could find a grave. But alas, after the resurrection, the first death is no more. The damned, in a sad sense, put on incorruption and immortality, they can never die and cease to feel their pains. They must always live a life ten thousand times worse than death, and there is no remedy. O you wicked men, where is your true love to your bodies, that you seem to be so tender of? I beseech you to mind your souls, and love your bodies better, than by sin to expose them to the vengeance of eternal fire. You see how in hell there is a deprivation of good, an infliction of evil, pain and torment. I add:

3. In hell there is an eternity of both, the deprivation will be without hope of restitution. And the torment will be without any end, without the least mitigation. Eternity is an amazing word. The thing itself is much more amazing! Who can see to the end of eternity! Who can see half way into eternity! Time is continually passing. But eternity never spends in the least. It is not capable of any diminution. After myriads of ages, it is still as bulky and whole as ever. If hell were ten thousand times hotter than it is, yet if it were only temporal punishment, and at last to end, it would be nothing in comparison. But since those that are thrown into it must lie in it forever, hell's eternity is the very hell of hell. In eternity, whether of joy or woe, there is *tota simul & perfecta possession*, the whole of it perfectly possessed at once. Hell is not parceled out to the damned, but they continually feel the whole of it. This is terrible. There is not the least part of the punishment that they are ever exempted from undergoing, but it is much more terrible that their suffering must be always, and never have a conclusion.

Divines have stretched their wits to represent eternity, that apprehensions of it might be more suitable and affecting, but were never able to reach it. We can no more comprehend eternity, than a nutshell can contain the whole ocean. Suppose that all this world were filled with sand, from the earth's center around, and up to the highest heaven. And once in a thousand years, one single sand should be taken away. How sad would it be to lie in torment, until the whole vast heap is gone! But after so many millions and millions of years, for the damned to be every bit as far from the end of their misery, as they were the very first moment they began to feel it. Here all words fall short, and I must conclude this thought in astonishment! Do not think that these are frightful things invented by us to scare you into better manners. When we warn and tell you of the eternity of hell's punishment, we speak the certain truth of the eternal God.

In the second place, I am to prove the doctrine. That those who will not turn to God will most certainly be turned into hell. The arguments to prove this are these.

1. The first shall be drawn from the wrath of God. This is "revealed from heaven against ungodliness and unrighteousness of men," (Romans 1:18). Those that are called to turn, and yet refuse, that wrath still abides on them. Unbelief and impenitency bind, as it were, all their sins fast on them, and they must needs remain under wrath also. "He that believeth not the son, shall not see life, but the wrath of God abideth on him," (John 3:36). No, wrath instead of being appeased, is increased, by comtempting the Gospel offer of God's favor and mercy in Christ. And where will unpacified

wrath at length issue? "A fire is kindled in mine anger, and it shall burn to the lowest hell," (Deuteronomy 32:22).

2. The second argument shall be drawn from the truth of God. He has threatened hell for the punishment of unconverted sinners. "The wicked shall be turned into hell, and all the nations that forget God," (Psalm 9:17). Let there never be so many of them, that hell has no room to hold them, and their multitude will not be any security. The truth of God is engaged to make all his promises good to the faithful, and also all his threatenings to the wicked. A man must believe the promises in order to the accomplishment of them. But though the threatenings are disbelieved, they will be fulfilled. And the greater the unbelief, the more certainly and sorely they will overtake and lay hold on the unbeliever.

The Lord is to be credited when he speaks, because he is a God that cannot lie. But when he adds his oath to his word, what he says is the more firmly to be assented to. His covenant of grace is confirmed by an oath, and when he could swear by no greater, he swore by himself. And his oath also confirms his threatenings of wrath. "And to whom swear he that they should not enter into his rest, but to them that believed not?" (Hebrews 3:18-19). So we see that they could not enter in because of unbelief.

3. Another argument to prove that unconverted sinners shall be turned into hell, shall be drawn from their present impunity. Escaping scot-free now, we may conclude the greater certainty of a future reckoning. Those that will not turn to God, we see that many of them are in good health, at ease, enjoying peace and plenty, and sentence against their evil works not now being executed, and they are fully set to do evil because of this. It is reasonable to believe there will be, and it is very righteous that there should be a terrible sentence of condemnation, and that sentence put in execution on them in the other world.

4. Those that will not turn to God at the Gospel call shall be turned into hell, for they slight the only Savior. Christ calls himself a door. So he has been this from the beginning of the world. So he will be this to the end of it. There is no door through which hell can be escaped, but this. Unconverted sinners "will not come to him that they may have life," (John 5:40) therefore they are unavoidably seized by eternal death. Corruptible things, as silver and gold, they know how to value, but the precious blood of Christ is not prized, and not being sprinkled with the blood of Christ, our Passover, who was sacrificed for us. The destroyer has power over them, and they fall into eternal perdition.

Chapter 9: Turn to God or Turn into Hell

In the third place, I am to vindicate the righteousness of God in dealing with this, and eternally punishing those that will not turn to him. And *here*:

1. Let the majesty and greatness of God be considered, against whom all sin is committed. How much greater a crime is it to strike a prince on the throne, than to strike a peasant! How much is sin made greater, being committed against the highest majesty of all, who is infinitely superior to all other powers. "O Lord, my God, thou art very great, thou art clothed with honor and with majesty!" (Psalm 104:1). "Great is the Lord, and greatly to be praised, and his greatness is unsearchable," (Psalm 145). Sin is a transgression of a law, enacted by the King of heaven. And is indeed a disowning of his sovereign authority, as if he had no right to rule the sinner. Think of the infinite distance between God, who is offended, and man, who is the offender, and how much sin offends. For it disowns his government, and strikes at his very Being. For the sinner wishes there were no God to be subject to. I say, think of all this, and you will perceive that sin deserves everlasting punishment. The carnal mind thinks hell to be too much for a sinner to feel, because it measures God by itself, and thinks too little of the glorious Jehovah.

2. Sinners can never satisfy that which is due for their iniquities by all that they suffer themselves. Therefore their

punishment in hell is justly endless. No mere creature can make satisfaction for sin. If Christ the Mediator had not been over all, God blessed forever, by his death and his sufferings, he would never have made peace. His Godhead put a real and infinite value on the price he paid, and made it sufficient for our redemption. The damned in hell cannot satisfy the justice of God for their transgressions. Therefore they justly are kept as eternal prisoners there. It is above five thousand years ago, that the evil angels were cast down to hell. By the punishment they have undergone, have they made any satisfaction for their offenses? No, no, still they have continued in their enmity, and deserved more punishment. And from Satan's utter alienation from God and all goodness, we may infer that hell is not a place to mend any. But sin is heightened. Those that were bad on earth, become worse in hell, and are unalterably confirmed in evil.

3. The punishment of sin in hell is justly eternal, because sin is insatiable. Suppose a sinner could live in this world to eternity, there is corruption enough in his nature, to make him an offender of God to eternity. If he was forever to live on the earth, he would be an everlasting transgressor. If the carnal heart would only speak out, that would be its language. "I would desire no other, no greater happiness, than that I might live here forever, that I might sin here forever."

This insatiable nature of sin, this inclination and desire of the sinner, is known to the heart searcher. Therefore the punishment he inflicts is very righteous, though it is everlasting.

4. For the vindication of the righteousness of God, take notice of what has been offered to sinners, and rejected. Christ is offered. His justifying righteousness, his unsearchable riches; all his fullness, all the benefits which he has purchased at so dear a price, and yet the offer is made light of. How much is condemned and how much of sin there is to contempt! The blessed God in the glorious Gospel calls to sinners to turn to him. And what does he offer? His own all-sufficient self. "I myself am yours, if you will turn to me, and become sincerely mine. I will be a God to you, all my attributes shall be before you. I will be your shield, and your exceedingly great reward, and your portion forever!" Now for a sinner to turn a deaf ear to all this, is such a sin that deserves the eternal loss of what is offered. And the feeling of everlasting wrath is just, since such infinite and everlasting goodness has been despised. I might also add, that the sinner is told of this eternal punishment beforehand. Therefore if his lusts are so dear, that he will venture to be damned, rather than to part with them, when those lusts that war against his soul have quite undone him, and brought him down to hell, he must blame himself,

because when warned of hell and wrath, he would not fear and flee from it.

I now come to the application. I begin with some inferences that may be drawn from the *doctrine:*

1. If sinners that will not turn, shall be brought down to hell, certainly sin is another kind of thing than is commonly imagined. O! sin, how much are you mistaken! You are very little understood on earth! In heaven you are better understood by the saints, and they are fully glad that they are quite rid of you! In hell you are better understood by sinners, and they must groan forever under your weight! O all of you, study hell more, if you would know sin more fully. God's severity towards man for sin, argues it to be a very vast evil. I am persuaded that all the men on earth, that all the saints and angels in heaven, since they cannot comprehend the greatness and goodness of God, neither can they comprehend all the evil that sin is, he alone is the competent Judge of what punishment it is due. O exceedingly sinful sin! (Romans 7:13). You cannot be called by so bad a name, as your own is!

2. Learn from this the misery of unconverted sinners. Are there none unconverted here? I wish there were not. Are there not many unconverted in this place? I fear there are. Seriously consider in what state you are in. You walk on the brink of hell. You eat and drink on the brink of hell, in your

Chapter 9: Turn to God or Turn into Hell

shops, at the exchange, you are still on the brink of hell. When you lie down at night, you sleep on the brink of hell. O! what hearts are yours, that you can sleep securely! Is such a perilous state to be rested in? In such danger, and depths of misery, how should you cry to the Lord for mercy. David's words are proper for a sinner to make use of. "Have mercy on me, O Lord, according to thy loving kindness, and according to the multitude of thy tender mercies, blot out my transgressions," (Psalm 51:1).

3. Here I infer, that those who refuse to turn to God are certainly besides themselves, else the broken cisterns would not draw them away from the Fountain of living waters. And a little gain and pleasure would not make them venture to lie in unquenchable flames. God says, "turn ye, turn ye!" Will you turn, or will you not? If you will, you shall live. If you will not, where are your wits? You are out of them in the worst sense of all. The Lord now says, "Turn," if you will not hear and obey, at last he will say, "Depart," and that word you must obey, and be forced away from him into everlasting burnings.

4. Shall sinners be turned into hell. Then their prosperity is not to be envied or admired. It has been a custom in some places to grant to condemned malefactors, a liberty to enjoy their pleasures and delights a few days before their

execution. But alas, what did these signify to those that were to die a few days after? A fair representation of the condition of the wicked! They are perhaps gaudily clothed, and daintily fed, and have more than the heart could wish for. But this prosperity is very short, that stand in slippery places, and quickly fall. "They are brought to destruction as in a moment, and utterly consumed with terrors," (Psalm 73:18-19). The ungodly do very much need our pity. But nothing that they have is worth our envy.

5. Here I infer the happiness of sincere converts. Many temporal evils may be their exercise at present, but they shall never feel hell's eternal torments. "There is therefore no condemnation to them that are in Christ Jesus, who walk not after the flesh, but after the Spirit," (Romans 8:1). Whatever the times are, in eternity, and to eternity, it will be well with them. If hell was ransacked all over, you might find professors, preachers, princes, and nobles there. You might find worldly wise, and worldly wealthy to be a great many, but not one true convert among the whole number. Converts are reconciled to God by the blood of Christ, and are safe and happy. Hell is a dreadful place, and has a very wide door. But who has the key of it? The key is not in Satan's, but in Christ's keeping. "I am he that liveth, and was dead, and behold I am alive forevermore, Amen, and I have the keys of hell and of

death," (Revelation 1:18) that converted bodies may come out of the grave. He will keep the door of hell fast shut, that converts shall never be thrown into there.

Use 2, of exhortation. That you would all consider more seriously and believe more heartily in this doctrine of hell. Often think of the loss sustained, and of the torment felt there. It was the advice of Chrysostom, "Let us not fly the remembrance of hell torment, that we may never be tormented there." The believing consideration of hell's punishment will have many good effects.

1. Hereby the deceitfulness of sin will be discovered. The deceitfulness of sin hardens you. "Exhort one another daily, while it is called today, lest any of you be hardened through the deceitfulness of sin," (Hebrews 3:13). Sin pretends to consult your ease, your safety, your satisfaction, your gain, your pleasure. Think seriously of hell, and all these will be found to be vain pretenses. O! how very false a thing sin is! First you must prove hell to be desirable, before you can prove that sin is worthy to be loved and served.

2. The remembrance of hell will be a great preservative against the tempter. Evil angels are great enemies to the good Word of God; especially those who are displeased at sermons concerning Christ and hell. They are unwilling that men should know the destruction that sin has brought them in

danger of, unwilling that they should hear of a Savior and Deliverer. Think of hell whenever you find the devil tempting. He endeavors to hide hell from your eyes, that he may lead you there securely. Satan tells the intemperate man, that makes himself a beast by excessive drinking. That this is the way to exhilarate and cheer his spirits, a remedy against care and sorrow, and a means to make him merry. But he would not have the drunkard think of hell, nor of the dreadful cup of God's indignation without mixture, that will be put into his hand at the last day. Satan tells the defrauding, over-reaching knave that he will be a great gainer by his subtlety. But he hides hell from him, where none of his gain remains, and where eternal happiness, and an immortal soul are lost forever. Satan tells the filthy wretch of the pleasures to be found in the embraces of the well favored harlot. But he conceals that going to her house, his feet go down to death, and his steps will soon take hold on hell. It would be wisdom in you, and in all, to see how sin and hell are joined together. It would make the tempter lose his labor. If you would ever remember that in tempting you to sin, he does in effect only persuade you to be willing to be destroyed forever.

3. The serious consideration of hell will quicken you to cry for mercy. On the sight of hell's misery, how desirable will mercy be in your eyes! You will pray for this with all prayer.

God will find you in the congregation, in the family, and in the closet, making your fervent supplications. And mercy will be your great suit. God delights in showing mercy, (Micah 7:18). The thoughts of hell will make you see how much you need it, and such do not fail to obtain it.

4. The remembrance of hell will contribute much to your steadfastness in religion. It will fortify and arm you against the fear of man. How little is it that the greatest man, that the *most* of men, can do to you? To fall into the hands of mortal men, that can only kill the body, which is no great matter. But to fall into the hands of the living God is fearful. Hark at what our Lord says, "I say unto you my friends, be not afraid of them that kill the body, and after that have no more that they can do. but I will forewarn you whom you shall fear. fear him who after he hath killed, hath power to cast into hell. yea, I say unto you, fear him," (Luke 12:4-5). Yes, he is indeed worthy to be feared! It was a saying of one, *all punishments are overcome by the fear of greater punishments.* When you are called forth to bear testimony to Christ and to his truth, before a sinful and adulterous generation. Though you see wracks and wheels, though you see flames and furnaces of scalding lead, do not be frightened at the matter. The grace and comfort of the Spirit of Christ shall be sufficient to carry you through these pains. And these are nothing compared to the vengeance

of eternal fire, which will be inflicted on those that draw back to perdition.

Use 3, of direction. How this whole congregation may escape the damnation of hell. I hope every eye is broad awake; and should not every ear be open, and every heart be exceedingly attentive, when directions concerning this are given? The directions are *these*:

1. If you would escape hell, think of hell, the effect of sin, so long, until you utterly fall out with sin, and the cause of sin. Sin is the only way that leads to hell, shun that way and you are safe. Depart from evil, and though you possibly may become a prey in this world, Satan will not make a prey of you. If sin had never entered into the world, none in the world would have been turned into hell. If neither men nor angels had sinned against God, there would have been no such thing as hell in existence. O! View the flames that are so furious, and that will last forever, and then consider that sin is that which kindled them, and the demerit of sin is so infinitely great, that it hinders them from ever being quenched. Does your pride expose you to damnation? Never be proud again. Will your earthly mindedness bring you to hell? O! cease your loving the world, and thing things that are in the world! (1 John 2:15). Will any sin that rules in you, and that you are willingly subjected to, reign to death, and ruin you forever? O! be

Chapter 9: Turn to God or Turn into Hell

unwilling that any sin should reign any longer. And if sin is out of your will, it is out of the throne. Cry with David, "Order my steps in thy Word, and let no iniquity have the dominion over me," (Psalm 119:133). You must be weary over sin's dominion, as well as fear hell's damnation. You must not think to go to heaven, and carry your beloved lusts along with you there. If you are resolved to hold fast to these, you will go to hell together with them.

2. If you would escape hell, take notice how the door of hope is open to the very worst of you. Those that have gone far down hell's road, and are within a step of the burning lake, it is possible for them to be caught as firebrands out of the burning. The door is open today, I advise you to enter presently. I cannot assure you that it will stand open until tomorrow. "While it is called today, harden not your hearts," (Hebrews 3:8). Though you are fallen by your iniquities, yet if you will now return to the Lord, there is hope for the very worst of you. Past sins shall all be buried, if there is a present conversion. Redemption is plenteous, and that should abundantly encourage all to hope and turn. "Let Israel hope for with the Lord there is mercy, and with him there is plenteous redemption, and he shall redeem Israel from all his iniquities," (Psalm 130:7-8).

3. If you would escape hell, you must be sure to look to Jesus. Lord Jesus! Turn every eye to you, and cause every heart to open and receive you! Those that were stung with the fiery serpents, lived notwithstanding, if they looked to the brazen serpent. Those that are in danger of hell, and have very well deserved it, shall be delivered from it, if by faith they look to Christ. "Look unto me, and be ye saved, all ye ends of the earth," (Isaiah 45:22). Look to him for pardon, look to him for converting, cleansing, and renewing grace; look to him to be the Author, to be the Finisher of your faith also, (Hebrews 12:2). Christ was forsaken that you might graciously be received by the Lord. He was condemned to die, and suffered death on the cross, that you might be delivered from eternal death and condemnation. It is plain that this was his design. "For God so loved the world that he gave his only begotten Son, that whosoever believeth in him," should escape hell, and be brought safely to heaven, "should not perish, but have everlasting life," (John 3:16).

CHAPTER 10:
SIN THAT BESETS US

"And the sin that does so easily beset us," (Hebrews 12:1).

In the foregoing chapter, the apostle discourses concerning faith, which is the substance of things hoped for, the evidence of things not seen. He declares at large the wonderful and glorious effects that this faith produced in the saints under the Old Testament. By faith these believers denied themselves. By faith they conquered the whole world, not fearing its fiercest persecutions. Despising all its wealth, all its pleasures, all its glory, and confessed that they were strangers and sojourners on the earth. By faith they saw him that is invisible, and looked for a city, whose builder and maker is God.

Now in this verse where my text lies, the apostle applies to those believing Hebrews to whom he writes, what he had spoken concerning their faithful forefathers. These are called a cloud of witnesses. Concerning what were they witnesses of? Truly concerning the vanity of all things that are seen, that are only temporal. Witnesses concerning the excellency of those things that are not seen, which are eternal. They are styled a cloud, because of the greatness of their number. And perhaps there may be some allusion to the cloud in the wilderness, that guided Israel into Canaan. For though our Lord Jesus was typified in that cloud, and he is the unerring pattern and example whom we are bound to follow, yet in Scripture we are advised to also follow the footsteps of the flock. And in this very epistle, to be followers of those who through faith and patience inherit the promises.

The course of a Christian in this world is compared to a race. This race must by run, that the prize at the end of it may be obtained, and that we may run it the better, we are *removere prohibens*, to remove impediments, to lay aside every weight, and the sin that does so easily beset us.

In the words I have read, there are three things *observable*:

1. Here is an imitation of a danger and that is from sin. Sin and danger are inseperable. How can it choose but to be prejudicial to him that is guilty of it! You may as well imagine hell to be without pain, as sin to be without peril.

2. The greatest danger is from the sin that does most easily beset us. It is called by the Holy Spirit, τὴν εὐπερίστατον ἁμαρτίαν, (Heb. 12:1), the sin that hangs fastest about us. Some understand this to be original sin, the deprivation and corruption of nature. Some understand the carnal and ensnaring fear of man. The apostle arms the Hebrew saints against this, and would have them to be

courageous, and if called to it, resist even to blood, striving against sin. But by the sin that does most easily beset us, we may understand any sin that does so. Yet when we take notice of the master sin, which is most apt to prevail, we should by all means trace it to its original, and take notice of the corrupt fountain from which this strong and filthy stream proceeds.

3. Here is the way to be secured from danger, by laying aside every weight, and especially the greatest and the heaviest clog of all, the sin that most easily besets us. Cast away every transgression, so iniquity shall not be your ruin, but especially that which naturally you love best and more than all, because this, this, is most of all pernicious and destructive.

The *Doctrine* which I raise from these words is this. *Though all sin is to be cast away, the master sin is especially to be abandoned.*

In the handling of this doctrine I *shall:*

1. Prove that all sin is to be cast away.

2. I shall show you how the master sin may be known.

3. Produce the reasons, why this in a special manner is to be forsaken.

4. Lastly, make application.

In the first place I am to prove that *every* sin should be cast away, and the argument to convince you of this, is in the verse where my text lies. Every sin is a weight, and it is a most unreasonable thing that men should be fond of that which is burdensome and grievous. I shall demonstrate the weightiness of sin in these particulars:

1. Sin is a weight to a softened and sensible soul, though a stupid transgressor feels sin no more than a stone does a mountain that lies on it. Yet once the heart of stone is turned into a heart of flesh, sin presently becomes very burdensome. He that has a new heart and a new spirit given to him will have new and other apprehensions of sin, he will look on sin with sorrow, and himself with self-abhorrence. "A new heart will I give you, a new spirit will I put within you. Then shall ye remember your evil ways and your doings that have not been good, and shall loathe yourselves in your own sight for your iniquities and your abominations," (Ezekiel 36:26, 31). David could not make light of sin, when once convinced of its evil by the Spirit. He grieves because he had offended God. He fears his wrath that he had deserved, and earnestly implores compassion and favor. His sin lay very hard on him. "Mine iniquities are gone over my head, as an heavy burden, they are too heavy for me. I am troubled, I am bowed down greatly, I go mourning all the day long," (Psalm 38:4, 6).

2. Sin is a weight to the damned in hell. That is so, I know, but how weighty, I cannot express, no mind on earth is

able to conceive. Sin is the weight which has sunk all the souls that are there into that place of woe. And because sin will lie on them forever, they shall never be able to rise up under it. In hell there is a full, a general, an everlasting conviction that sin is heavy. If we could discourse with the rich man, who as the Gospel tells us is in hell, and ask him whether his gluttony, pride, contempt of God, hatred of holiness, are light or weighty? O, what would that tongue that cried out for a drop of water, answer to such a question? Surely none in hell can make light of sin which brought them there.

 3. Sin is a weight which burdens the whole creation. Hard-hearted man does not groan under it, when the whole creation besides him does. "The creatures were made subject to vanity, not willingly, but by reason of him who hath subjected the same in hope," "We know that the whole creation groaneth and travaileth in pain together even until now," (Romans 8:20, 22). And all these travailing pains are the effects of sin. Solomon, in the book of Ecclesiastes, uses several very significant expressions. "Vanity of vanities, all is vanity;" and "all things are full of labor; man cannot utter it." And again, there "are many things that increase vanity." When sin entered into the world, it made a sad alteration in it, well may the creatures groan under it. And though their pains are terrible right now, pains of travail here on earth, yet because

such pains are hopeful, and will issue in a restoration, which will certainly be, for God has said it. He has told us this much, that the "creature shall be delivered from the bond of corruption, into the glorious liberty of the children of God," (Romans 1:21). But the manner of this restoration, he has not told us. God's silence should repress inquisitive curiosity.

4. Sin was found to be a weight by Jesus the Mediator. He undertook (and it was well for us that he did) to bear this burden, and no shoulders but his could have born it. But when he bore it, how he groaned under it! This put him into agony, this made him sweat, and sweat drops of blood. This made him to cry out, "my soul is exceedingly sorrowful, even to death," and "My God, my God, why hast thou forsaken me?" O! sinner, it was your sin and the sins of all the others whom I save, that lay so hard on me. "All we like sheep have gone astray, we have turned everyone to his own way, and the Lord hath laid on him the iniquity of us all," (Isaiah 53:6). If the man Christ Jesus had not been the eternal Son of God, he could have never born such a heavy load, as all the sins of his whole church laid on him at once together.

5. God himself complains of sin as a weighty thing, which he is very weary of. "Thou hast made me to serve with thy sins, and hast wearied me with thine iniquities," (Isaiah 43:24). And, "Behold I am pressed under you, as a cart is

Chapter 10: Sin that Besets Us

pressed that is full of sheaves," (Amos 2:13) Sin is a burden to the Almighty, though he is so rich and abundant in forbearance and long-suffering. No, sin will make duties to be a burden to him. "Bring no more vain oblations, your Sabbaths and calling of assemblies, I cannot away with, it is iniquity even the solemn meeting. Your new moons, and your appointed feasts, my soul hateth. they are a trouble to me," (Isaiah 1:13-14). And it is observable, when the Lord comes to a resolution to punish sinners, because of their transgressions, he speaks as one about to ease himself of a load. "Therefore thus saith the Lord, the Lord of hosts, the mighty one of Israel. Ah! I will ease me of my adversaries, and avenge me of my enemies," (Isaiah 1:24). If sin is such a weight, I advise all to be weary, and beg to be eased of it. He is a senseless fool indeed, who makes a mock of sin, and still goes on to add to his own burden.

In the second place, I shall show you how the master sin may be known. And here I will premise these three *things:*

1. All sin that is allowed of, may truly be said to reign, where it is allowed. A man that willfully continues in the commission of any sin, is certainly the servant of it, whatever it is. It is the misery of the unregenerate, that they have, *tot Dominos quot vitia*, so many lusts, so many Lords.

2. There is a particular sin in many people, which prevails more than any other. In the natural body there are all the humors, yet one commonly is predominant, and the denomination is from that. So it is in the body of sin. Though there is a mass of all corruption, yet there may be some special corruption, that has the greatest strength and prevalence. In Scripture this is called the sweet sin, in which the greatest delight is taken, compared to a sweet morsel under the tongue. "Though wickedness is sweet in his mouth, though he hide it under his tongue, though he spare it and forsake it not." Yet at last it proves extremely bitter, deadly as the very gall of asps within him.

3. There are some in whom several sins are so predominant, that it is hard to determine which is the master. Some have so hot an anger, and so hot and furious a lust, that you cannot so easily judge which of these is hottest. No, in some, sins that seem very contrary to one another, yet in several respects, they both prevail. Many a man is liberal and profuse, as to his ornaments and clothing. He spends freely in the sumptuous furnishing of his table. Hand and purse are open, if he is in riotous company. Yet if you ask this man for only a little, for good use. Tell him that the members of Christ are many of those who are needy, and that he who gives to the poor, lends to the Lord. Here he is strangely covetous and

Chapter 10: Sin that Besets Us

close-fisted. With these things premised, I shall discover the master sin.

1. That is a master sin, to which the constitution most strongly inclines. Those that are of a sanguine complexion are inclined to lasciviousness, voluptuousness, and an airy frothiness of spirit, which is a great hindrance to the serious impressions. In the choleric, passion and anger are apt to prevail, and to hurry them to revengeful words and actions, not considering what injury they do to others, and how much more to themselves. The melancholic are prone to envy, malice, discontent. The phlegmatic are prone to stupidity, carelessness, and sloth. Now Satan takes notice of the complexion, fails with the stream of it, and suits his bait to it and hereby has very great advantage. Though no sin has the dominion in believers, for they "are not under the law, but under grace," (Romans 6:14); yet the complexion sin is apt sometimes to master even those also. Therefore they had need to be watchful against it, and to take great care and pains to mortify it. The apostle Paul observes his own constitution, and makes conscience of keeping under his body that his temperament might not be his temptation. "I keep under my body, and bring it into subjection, lest by any means, when I have preached unto others, I myself should be cast away," (1 Corinthians 9:27).

2. That is a master sin, to which your callings and conditions make you most liable. Those that trade in the world, how apt are they through the corruption of their own hearts, to defraud and overreach, to get immoderate and dishonest gain. Hear that strict prohibition, "Let no man go beyond or defraud his brother in any matter, knowing that the Lord is the avenger of all such, as we also have forewarned you, and testified," (1 Thessalonians 4:6). How apt are they to venture on the sin of lying and equivocation, for advantage, and they teach and command their servants and children to follow their pernicious examples, as if earthly gain was so considerable, that it is no great matter how many souls are lost for the sake of it. Those that are rich in this world are prone to be "high-minded, and to trust in uncertain riches," (1 Timothy 6:17) to withhold the hire from the poor laborers. to live in "wantonness and pleasure," (James 5:1-3) to be full and deny God, and say, "Who is the Lord?" Those that are poor in the world are prone to steal; (all unjust dealing is stealing, an unjust action makes a man a thief in God's account) and "to take the name of God in vain," (Proverbs 30:9).

3. That is the master sin, which the sinner is most unwilling to be brought to light, and cannot bear to be reproved for. We read, "Everyone that doth evil, hateth the light, neither cometh to the light, lest his deeds should be

reproved," (John 3:20) But of all others, he cannot endure to be reproved for the sin that easily besets him, and that he loves most. He tramples the pearl of reproof under his feet, and is ready to turn again, and rend the reprover. John the Baptist was a burning and a shining light. Herod the king heard him, some of his exhortations and doctrines went down with Herod, and produced a partial reformation. At length John the Baptist comes home, and strikes at the master sin, tells Herod of his Herodias, and that it was "not lawful for him to have his brother's wife." This was not to be tolerated, the king counted the prophet too bold to meddle with his beloved lust. He hears him no longer. He first puts him into prison, and afterwards puts him to death, and so was this burning and shining light extinguished, (Matthew 6:17, 27).

4. The master sin, conscience, when awakened by distress, is very apt to accuse the sinner of, and furiously to fly in his face for. Conscience, though it sleeps in a calm, usually awakes in a storm. When death-threatening affliction lies hard on the sinner, and he looks beyond death to judgment, and into eternity. Then conscience speaks plainly, rebukes boldly, and especially the master sin makes it very clamorous. Envy was a sin predominant in Joseph's brothers, for they could not bear the thoughts of his future advancement. They sold him as a slave, to prevent his being exalted over them, as

was presigned by his dreams. Many years after, God calls for a famine on the land. The brothers go down into Egypt to buy food, and Joseph seizes them, deals hardly with them, and they are in great distress. Conscience now awakens, and with great terror it flies in their faces, and their envy and cruel dealing with Joseph their brother, comes to remembrance with great anguish and trouble. "They said one to another, we are very guilty concerning our brother. in that we saw the anguish of his soul, when he besought us and we would not hear. therefore is this distress come on us, therefore behold also is his blood required," (Genesis 42:21-22). Conscience comments on affliction, and has its terrible glosses. These blows are given to you for your secret filthiness, for your intemperance, for your injustice, for your earthly mindedness, for your doing the work of God heartlessly and negligently! Observe what conscience now says, for it takes notice of the master sin.

5. That is a master sin, which when the sinner is almost persuaded to be a convert, hinders him from being a convert altogether. That Jacob might have corn, he was content that ten of his sons should go and fetch it. But how loathe was he to let Benjamin go! When a sinner is convinced of the necessity of conversion, he may consent to part with two or three or ten sins. But that which is most beloved, he

Chapter 10: Sin that Besets Us

hugs still, he and that sin must never part. When the soul is ready to be espoused to Christ, this sin stands up and forbids the banes. We read of a young man in the Gospel, soberly inclined. He saw the necessity of eternal life and the value of it. He comes to Jesus and says, "Good Master, what shall I do that I may inherit eternal life?" Our Lord tells him of the commands, the young man is glad of this, for as to the letter of the second table precepts. He had been a strict observer of them all from his youth. At length, our Lord, who knew that love to the world was his master sin, bids him to go and sell all that he had on earth, and follow him, and he should have more enduring treasure in heaven. But his love to the world hindered his believing and conversion, and he goes away "very sorrowful, for he was very rich," (Matthew 19:21-22). His riches were very unreasonably and excessively loved, for he cleaves to mammon, and leaves the only Savior!

6. That is a master sin, which pretends most highly to consult the sinner's safety, gain, and pleasure. To be safe, to be advantaged, and delighted, are things very taking to human nature. Pretenses are prevalent this way, but all of sin's pretenses are vain. When our Lord commands that the right eye should plucked out, and the right hand cut off. The meaning is not that Christianity binds us cruelly to dismember ourselves. Indeed, the abuse of our members is

severely forbidden, but our members themselves are not to be parted with, but employed after in a holy manner. That therefore which our Lord intends is this, either, that we should be as without an eye, to behold vanity and tempting objects; as without a hand to work that which is evil. Or, that though sin is naturally as dear to us as our right eye, as seemingly necessary as our right hand. Yet we must part with it, and not spare it to the hazard and ruin of ourselves forever, (Matthew 5:29-30). I might also add, that sinners are apt above all to wish that the master sin was no sin at all. And because the law forbids it, they hate the law, and the motions of their wicked hearts toward it are more strong and violent. And here is a notable difference between an unsanctified and a sanctified heart. The unsanctified heart wishes that the law was less holy, that sins were not sins. But the heart that is sanctified, does not desire the law to be less strict and pure, but that itself was more pure, and more conformed to a law that is so good and excellent. It does not desire a liberty to commit sin, but that all the remaining lusts of the flesh were more thoroughly mortified.

In the third place I am to produce the reasons why this master sin ought to be especially abandoned.

1. Because this is God's principal enemy. All sin is against him, but this is a special provocation in the eyes of his

holiness and glory. The apostle tells us that love is the greatest grace. And Christ himself says that love is the first and greatest commandment. The master sin, which is most beloved, which takes away the affection of the heart, which God chiefly requires, must needs provoke him to great jealousy. This is the presumptuous sin, it is greatly offensive, for deservedly it is called the "great transgression," (Psalm 19:13).

2. The master sin should be abandoned, because in a special manner, it separates between God, and the soul that is guilty of it. Sin has many bad effects, but a worse cannot be named than this, "Your iniquities have separated between you and your God, and your sins have hid his face from you that he will not hear," (Isaiah 59:2). Let the saints in heaven speak what it is to see the face of God! O! the evil that is in sin, which causes the face of God to be hidden from the sinner! Every sin may be compared to a cloud. But the sin which most easily besets us is the blackest, the darkest cloud of all, which most totally deprives us of the light of God's countenance.

3. If the master sin is not abandoned, no other sin whatsoever can truly be repented of. A man may indeed abstain from some sins, but he does not abstain from them, as sins, and because they are displeasing to God, but because they are contrary to his will, and because they hinder

communion with God. If he did, then certainly he would keep himself from the beloved sin, which is principally hateful to God, and the grand obstruction of fellowship with him.

4. The master sin should be abandoned, because this is so great a grief to the Holy Spirit of God. How often does he tell the false professor of his lying tongue, and the unjust professor of his unrighteous dealing! The good Spirit vouchsafes to strive with very wicked men, and moves them to hate the sin which they unreasonably love to their own ruin. But if sin is still loved, the Spirit is grieved and vexed. And is it safe to grieve and vex the *sanctifier*, the *comforter*? No. Read what follows on vexing the Spirit, "But they rebelled, and vexed his Holy Spirit, therefore he was turned to be their enemy, and he fought against them.

5. The master sin should be abandoned, because it is this that chiefly keeps the Lord Jesus out of the throne. Why do so many say in their hearts, "we will not have Christ to reign over us?" The reason is because they are resolved that their fleshly and worldly lusts shall still rule there. And if Christ does not rule, it is in vain to expect that he will save, for he is the "Author of eternal salvation to those that obey him," (Hebrews 5:9). No, as he will not save those that will not be subject to him, so he has threatened to slay them. As "for those mine enemies, that would not that I should reign

Chapter 10: Sin that Besets Us

over them, bring them forth, and slay them before me," (Luke 19:27).

CHAPTER 11:

APPLICATION TO WILLINGLY HAVE SUCH SIN DISCOVERED

In the last place, I come to the application, and there are three *uses*:

Use 1, by way of examination. Try yourselves, whether you are willing to abandon the sin that so easily besets you, and for your help in this matter, I would ask *you*:

1. Are you willing to have this sin, whatever it is, to be discovered? Are you willing that God should signify to you, what it is in you that most of all displeases him? Job professes that he "covered not his transgression, as Adam, by hiding his iniquity in his bosom," (Job 31:33). He that hides sin, loves it. He that pleads for sin, is a servant, a slave to it. The defense of sin is worse than the offense itself. Can you come to God and say, "Lord, I open my heart to you. Search, ransack here. Let no sin lie concealed! Let not so much as one be spared, but especially the master sin, which is my greatest enemy, as well as yours."

2. Are you willing to hear all the evil the Word speaks against the master sin? If so, this would argue that it is no

Chapter 11: Application to Willingly have such Sin Discovered

longer loved. It is a sign of malice towards our neighbor, if we are glad to hear all the evil that is spoken of him, and all the reproach that is cast on him. It is a sign of hatred to sin, when we like to have it discovered, when we like that its deceitful and damnable nature should be represented, and the falseness, foulness, and filthiness of it should be laid open and naked. Sin is so great an evil, that there cannot be too much evil spoken of it. It is so great an enemy, that you can never too faithfully and plainly be warned against it.

3. Do you apprehend your greatest danger to be from your master sin and therefore continually endeavor the mortification of it? The king of Syria gave this commission to his army, "Fight neither against small nor great, save only with the King of Israel." What? Were all others to be spared? No certainly, many Israelites fell in the battle, but there was a principle design to take at least, if not to cut off the king of Israel. All sin deserves your hatred, no sin is so small an enemy as that you may safely spare it. But the master sin is the chief foe, therefore its destruction should chiefly be designed. That man that is an enemy to his master sin desires that it may be still weakened by all means. Oh, says he, that every mercy may help to kill it, leading me to repentance of it! That every stroke of the rod may help to strike it more dead! That every sermon may give this sin a blow! That I may obtain more strength

against it by every prayer! That every time I come to the table of the Lord, this sin may be in a greater measure crucified!

Use 2, of exhortation. And of this there are two *branches*:

I shall speak to sinners that are under the full power of their master sin. Then I shall speak to saints, in whom there are too great remainders of it.

1. I am to speak to sinners who are under the full power of their master sin. It is told concerning Agrippa, the mother of *Nero Caesar*, that it was told to her by an oracle, that her son should be the emperor of Rome, but afterwards should kill his own mother. Agrippa replies, *Occidat, mode imperit!* Let him kill me, so he does but reign. O it is the language of all presumptuous sinners concerning their master lusts, "Let them but reign, no matter though they are our damnation and destruction!" But what do you see in sin, or in its wages, that any of you should be thus fond of its service? What good reason can be given, why sin should have one slave in this whole congregation, or in the whole world? I earnestly exhort you to lay aside every weight, but especially the sin that most easily besets you. Arguments to persuade are these:

1. Consider, the master sin is the strongest hold of Satan. While sin keeps us its dominion, Satan holds fast his possession. This sin is your most deadly disease, and the

strongest cord, in which the devil binds you and leads you captive at his pleasure.

2. The master sin is the great hindrance of the efficacy of the means of grace. This makes the preacher's pains, lost labor. This makes the mercies and afflictions to be lost on you. This makes you to lose all the duties you perform.

3. This master sin is not without its train of smaller sins. A great person, especially a crowned head, is not without a great many that attend him! A master sin has a great attendance. Many lusts are subservient to this main one, that the greater and more plentiful provision may be made for the fulfilling of it. How great is your danger, who has so many enemies lodging in you, and lording it over you!

4. Suppose, this master sin was alone, this would be enough to ruin you. If a pistol discharged at the heart, and the small bullet entered there, it kills as certainly as if there were a thousand cannons discharged at a man at once. One sin suffered to rule in your heart is sufficient even if there were no more, effectually and eternally to ruin you.

5. The master sin wars against your soul most dangerously, and wounds most deeply. And after it has ruined you, O! with what anguish it will be relented on in the lowest hell! This will be your heaviest load there! You will remember how deaf you were to all counsel to cast it away, and how

great your madness was, in taking the most pleasure in that, which proves the cause of the greatest, even everlasting sorrow and vexation. O! be so wise as to change your old master, sin, and let Christ become your Lord.

2. I am to speak to saints, in whom there are too great remainders of the sin that was once their master. I exhort you more effectually and thoroughly to mortify it. Pray consider,

1. If this sin frequently prevails, it will keep you very low in grace. Faith will be weak, hope will be dampened, love will be cool. and the whole inward man will woefully languish.

2. As you will be weak in grace, so will you be low in comfort. When temptations are yielded to, conscience will be disquieted, peace will be disturbed. your pride, passion, carnal affections prevailing, will make your heart too much like the troubled. "But the wicked are like the troubled sea, when it cannot rest, whose waters cast up mire and dirt," (Isaiah 57:20).

3. The prevalence of this easily besetting sin will hinder you from being so serviceable to your great and gracious Lord. It will make his work to be neglected. and when done, to be done too negligently. You will be sorry servants, and you will have very sorry services. The more sanctified you are, the fitter you are for your Masters use, (2

Timothy 2:21) but sin makes you unfit, and more unable and unwilling to serve him.

4. This sin will make you to shine less in your lives. It will fill your conversations, and hinder you from adorning the Gospel. O! keep unspotted, and walk exactly as in the day, that you "may be blameless and harmless children of God, without rebuke, in the midst of a crooked and perverse nation, and that you may shine as lights in the world," (Philippians 2:15).

5. This sin may cause your mind to be set in a cloud. It may fill you with doubts when you are dying, and that will be very dreadful. You may be terribly frightened with the fears of hell, when you are just at heaven's gate. Therefore be upright, keep yourselves from the iniquity that so easily besets you. That you may be more useful in your lives, have the stronger and more lively hope in death, and that your end, when it comes, may be more perfect peace.

Use 3, of direction. How the sin which most easily besets you may be laid aside.

1. Pray for a clean heart, (Psalm 51:10). David, having been overcome by a strong corruption, and having done a deed that was very foul, cries for a purer heart, a more right and constant Spirit. He knew that to purge the fountain was the way to have the streams clean. Go to God for a new heart,

which he has promised, and will give to all who prize and desire such a heart. Strike at the root of sin in the heart, then the branches, and this top branch, the master sin will wither.

2. Seriously lay to heart how much the sin that naturally is more beloved, deserves your hatred. Hated sin is so weak that it can ruin none. It is the love of sin that gives it power, and as it were, puts a sword into its hand to slay you.

3. Resist the very first stirrings of this sin in you. I believe if David, as soon as ever he beheld from his palace, the beauteous Bathsheba, had presently turned away his eyes, and had fallen on his knees, and gone to prayer, he would have overcome the temptation. Sin is more weak at the beginning. Our Lord's counsel is, "Watch and pray, that ye enter not into temptation," (Matthew 26:41).

4. If you would abandon the master sin, pray much for the contrary grace. Is pride your master sin? Pray much for humility. Is passion your master sin? Pray much for patience and for the meekness and gentleness of Christ. Is love to the world your master sin? Pray that you may rise with Christ, and love and mind a better world. better honors, better pleasures, a more lasting wealth than this world can yield.

5. Let the word of God, which forbids and threatens this master sin, be carefully hid in your heart. This word may be in your mouth, you may talk of it. It may be in your mind,

you may have a notional knowledge of it. Now, it may go further, and be in your conscience, and be thought of in the very act of sin. But if it is in your heart, if your will and affections are taken with it, then it will be an effectual preservation against iniquity. "Thy Word have I hid in my heart, that I might not sin against thee," (Psalm 119:11).

6. Improve the death of our Lord Jesus. Bring the sin which does easily beset you to the cross of Christ. No sin truly dies, except on Christ's cross. "They that are Christ's have crucified the flesh with the affections and lusts," (Galatians 5:24). They are never mortified but by being crucified. How can the old Adam die, except on the cross of the second Adam? "Knowing this, that our old man is crucified with him, that the body of sin might be destroyed, that hereforth we should not serve sin," (Romans 6:6).

7. Call in the Spirit's aid. He can make the Word sharp as a two-edged sword to pierce the heart, and to slay the strongest sin there. He glorifies Christ, and can draw you to him, and enable you by faith to derive grace from him, sufficient to help you against the most powerful corruptions. He can kill the sin that is hardest to be slain. He can "mortify all the deeds of the body," (Romans 8:13). "The strongest members of the earth," (Colossians 3:5) and he can seal you to the day of redemption. AMEN

www.ingramcontent.com/pod-product-compliance
Lightning Source LLC
Chambersburg PA
CBHW022156080426
42734CB00006B/453